# Enemies of the People under Stalinism

# Enemies of the People under Stalinism

Alexey Vinogradov
Albert Pleysier

HAMILTON BOOKS
*an imprint of*
*Rowman & Littlefield*
*Lanham • Boulder • New York • London*

Published by Hamilton Books
An imprint of The Rowman & Littlefield Publishing Group, Inc.
4501 Forbes Boulevard, Suite 200, Lanham, Maryland 20706
www.rowman.com

86-90 Paul Street, London EC2A 4NE, United Kingdom

British Library Cataloguing in Publication Information Available

**Library of Congress Cataloging-in-Publication Data**

Names: Vinogradov, A. V. (Alekseĭ Vladimirovich), author. | Pleysier, Albert Jan, 1948– author.
Title: Enemies of the people under Stalinism / Alexey Vinogradov, Albert Pleysier.
Description: Lanham : Hamilton Books, an imprint of Rowman & Littlefield, [2023] | Includes bibliographical references and index. | Summary: "In this book the author's explore the lives of Soviet citizens who were declared "enemies of the people" during Joseph Stalin's dictatorship and were exiled from the Soviet Union, detained in city prisons, sent to prison labor camps located in Siberia, or executed"— Provided by publisher.
Identifiers: LCCN 2023024611 (print) | LCCN 2023024612 (ebook) | ISBN 9780761874065 (cloth) | ISBN 9780761874072 (paperback) | ISBN 9780761874102 (epub)
Subjects: LCSH: Exiles—Soviet Union—Biography. | Political prisoners—Soviet Union—Biography. | Political persecution—Soviet Union. | Soviet Union—Politics and government—1936–1953. | Soviet Union—Politics and government—1917–1936. | False imprisonment—Soviet Union. | Deportation—Soviet Union.
Classification: LCC DK268.A1 V46 2023  (print) | LCC DK268.A1  (ebook) | DDC 947.084/2—dc23/eng/20230530
LC record available at https://lccn.loc.gov/2023024611
LC ebook record available at https://lccn.loc.gov/2023024612

# Contents

# Preface

Stalinism is the name that is used to identify the political and economic systems introduced and implemented by Joseph Stalin in the Soviet Union from the time that he became the supreme power in the Russian Communist Party in 1927 to his death in 1953. During those years, Stalin's economic policies turned the Soviet Union into an industrial giant with all industry under State control. The policies also brought about the collectivization of almost all of the agricultural land in the Soviet Union. Stalin adopted the theory of "socialism in one country" believing that it was possible to transform the Soviet Union into a socialist state without outside assistance. It was designed to be a state without the presence of Christianity or any other religious faith.

Those in the Soviet Union who disagreed with Stalin or who opposed his policies were arrested by Stalin's feared secret police organizations. The victims were either exiled from the Soviet Union, detained in city prisons, or sent to prison labor camps located in Siberia. No Soviet citizen was immune from arrest. This became evident during periods of time when Stalin purged the Russian Communist Party, the only recognized political party in the Soviet Union. The citizens who were declared guilty of the charges that were brought against them by the State, were labeled "enemies of the people." A victim' s family members, close relatives and friends would suffer serious consequences as well. No citizen felt safe. The chapters that follow the book's Introduction hold the personal accounts of Soviet citizens who were declared "enemies of the people" or who were related to "enemies of the people."

The lives of public figures, people that societies regard as important, have often been used by historians to record the events of the past. The events are seen through their eyes. The decisions that they made, the actions that they took and the influence that their decisions and actions had on future developments are described and explained. Revolutionary leaders such as Vladimir Lenin and Leon Trotsky and political leaders such as Joseph Stalin hold prominent places in the histories written about the birth and the early developments of the Soviet Union. Yet the experiences of the so-called lesser figures in society, women, men and children who are not mentioned by name in textbooks, are revealing and important illustrations of the events that occurred. Believing this to be true, the authors have taken the lives of former Soviet citizens who were interviewed by the authors and by others and they have placed the experiences of these people within historical settings. It is the hope of the authors that the lives of these people will give the reader a more personal description of life in the Soviet Union under the rule of Stalin.

# Acknowledgments

The drawing on the cover of the book is a portrait of Anna Akhmatova. She was identified with her first husband, Nikolai Gumilev, who was executed as an "enemy of the people." Anna, a poet by profession, was viewed with suspicion by the Soviet authorities. For many years, she was under constant government surveillance. The authors wish to thank Jane Pleysier for permission to use the drawing.

The authors also wish to thank Dr. Shahryar Heydari for formatting the text of the book, Sarah Bittner for designing the maps in the book and Mr. Bob Glass in matters concerning copy right laws and public domain.

Albert Pleysier dedicates the book to his Heavenly Father.

# Introduction

## *The Removal of the Romanov Dynasty*

At the dawn of the twentieth century, Russia was a politically authoritarian and economically backward power. The Romanov dynasty headed by Tsar Nicholas II regarded itself as a divine right monarchy, ruling with the help of a large bureaucracy and an army that was used toward territorial conquest and against rebellious subjects. A secret police force, that had made Siberia notorious as the site for Russian penal colonies, kept down dissent, but opposition against autocracy could not be quieted. Liberals, desiring to bring about political, social and economic reforms through peaceful and legal avenues, and revolutionaries, using terrorism, sought to overthrow Russian autocracy. The revolutionaries looked mostly to the Russian peasantry as their army of revolution and in the early nineteen hundreds the peasants as well as Russia's industrial workers would help bring about the fall of Russia's autocracy.

The people of imperial Russia faced major problems in the latter years of the nineteenth century. The peasant population increased by more than fifty percent between 1861 and 1900, mostly because of a high birthrate and a declining death rate, but the increase in the peasant population meant a reduction in the size of individual peasant land holdings. At the same time, Russia experienced the growth of a large-scale machine industry, which resulted in the emergence of an urban working class. Since industrialization was new to Russia, its workers labored under working conditions that were both unsafe and unhealthy. Wages were low and the average workday in a mill was from twelve to fourteen hours. The poor treatment from which the workers suffered, filled within them a feeling of deep discontent and militant consciousness.

In 1904–1905, Russia's imperial designs in eastern Asia culminated in a disastrous war against Japan. The Russo-Japanese War began with a Japanese surprise attack on the Russian naval squadron at Port Arthur in February

1904. Russia had leased Port Arthur from China in 1898 as part of its expansion efforts in East Asia and Manchuria. For years Russia's actions had troubled the Japanese. Russia had neither kept its promises to withdraw from eastern Asia nor had it acknowledged Japan's proposal to establish mutually acceptable spheres of influence. The war and the initial patriotism that the war evoked was welcomed by the tsar and his government. The war, however, was a disaster for Russia. In December 1904, the Russians surrendered Port Arthur and this was followed by Russian defeats in Manchuria and the annihilation of a large Russian fleet in Japanese waters.

When the reports of Russia's military defeats reached St. Petersburg, the workers in several factories in the capital city went on strike. A priest named George Gapon, hoping to deflect the workers from revolutionary ideas, urged the workers to petition the tsar to end the war, convene a constituent assembly, grant civil rights and establish an eight-hour workday. On Sunday morning, January 9, 1905, Father Gapon led a large group of industrial workers from various parts of the city toward the Winter Palace, the home of the tsar and his family in St. Petersburg. The marchers carried icons and sang "God save the tsar." As the petitioners approached the Winter Palace, they were ordered to halt. When they disregarded the order, the commander of the tsar's troops ordered his men to fire on the peaceful demonstrators. More than one hundred people were killed and many more were wounded.

The news of Bloody Sunday undermined the people's faith in the tsar and united them against autocracy. Throughout the empire, the massacre caused an angry uproar culminating in labor unrest, peasant insurrections, student demonstrations and mutinies in both the army and navy. Peasants, organizing themselves at the village level, discussed seizing the property of their landlords. Urban workers joined together in organizations that called for a general strike. The people who did participate in an organized strike demanded a democratic republic, the release of political prisoners and the disarming of the government's secret police. Most business and government offices were closed and Russia's economic life came to a halt.

The tsarist government managed to restore order in the fall of 1905 after agreeing to make political reforms. In October 1905, a month after the signing of the Treaty of Portsmouth which ended Russia's war with Japan, the tsar issued a manifesto that promised full civil liberties, a constitution and the creation of the Duma, an elected legislature with the power to enact laws. The October Manifesto was supposed to transform autocratic Russia into a constitutional monarchy. The constitution, which went into effect in 1906, stated that for a measure to become a law it had to be passed by the delegates in both houses of the Duma; however, the tsar retained absolute veto power. The tsar would also determine the duration of the Duma's sessions and he had the right to dissolve it at will if he set a date for new elections. Article 87 within the constitution allowed the executive to rule by decree. After the revolutionary crisis had passed, the tsarist government returned to its reactionary ways and restricted the authority of the Duma.

World War One hastened the decay that had been eating away at tsarist Russia for decades. In August 1914, Germany declared war on Russia. Initially, the declaration of war produced unity and patriotic resolve in Russia. Virtually the entire Duma pledged to support Russia's war efforts and voted for war appropriations. The people believed that the war was being fought to defend Russia and, in the cities, Russian patriotism became anti-German. The capital city was renamed Petrograd because its former name, St. Petersburg, sounded too German. The Russian high command dispatched two armies into Germany's eastern Prussia, but the push forward was only temporary. The German army responded quickly and, with their Austrian allies, drove the Russians out of Germany, through Poland and back into Russia. Hundreds of thousands of Russian soldiers lost their lives and Russian morale was seriously damaged. In the fall of 1915, Tsar Nicholas II left Russia's capital city to take personal command of the Russian armies.

In his absence from the capital city, the tsar placed effective control of the Russian government in the hands of his wife, Alexandra. By this time the tsarina had fallen under the influence of Grigori Rasputin, a semiliterate Siberian monk. To Alexandra, Rasputin was a holy man for he alone seemed able to stop through hypnosis the bleeding of her hemophiliac son, Alexis. Rasputin's influence over the tsarina made him an important power behind the throne and he did not hesitate to interfere in government affairs. Ministers were appointed and dismissed on a word from Rasputin. By late 1916, Rasputin's behavior had become so intolerable that three members of the high aristocracy, fearful for the survival of the monarchy, murdered the monk. His death would not make a difference; by this time public confidence in the tsar's government had disappeared. Two years of Russian military defeats, millions of military casualties, shortages of food and fuel in the cities, and government inefficiency and corruption had turned the people against the crown.

In March 1917, a series of strikes and demonstrations would bring to an end tsarist rule. In the month previous, the government had introduced bread rationing in Petrograd after the price of bread had soared. Many of the women who stood in lines waiting for bread were also factory workers who labored twelve-hour days. On March 8, a day celebrated since 1910 as International Women's Day, thousands of Petrograd women marched through the capital city demanding "peace and bread" and chanting "down with autocracy." Soon the women were joined by other workers and together they called for a general strike that succeeded in shutting down, on March 10, all the factories in the city. The tsarina informed her husband about these developments in a letter and the tsar responded by demanding the adjournment of the Duma and ordering the police and the troops stationed in Petrograd to disperse the striking crowds by shooting them if necessary. At first the soldiers obeyed, but soon a significant number of them joined the demonstrating crowds. On March 12, some members of the Duma formed a provisional committee to keep order. Hostility toward the crown and demonstrations against the government had already spread to other cities. Alone and helpless, Tsar Nicholas II followed the advice of his generals and abdicated on March 15 in favor of his younger brother, Michael. He, in turn, abdicated in favor of the Duma's provisional committee. By this time the members of the committee considered themselves a provisional government. The three-hundred-year reign of the Romanov dynasty ended and Russia ceased to be a monarchy.

At first the Provisional Government enjoyed considerable support both at home and abroad. It disbanded the tsarist police, granted amnesty to political prisoners and allowed exiles to return home. It repealed all limitations on freedom of speech, press and association. It abolished laws that discriminated against ethnic or religious groups. It announced plans for social reforms and promised to summon a democratically elected constituent assembly that was to establish a permanent government by giving Russia a constitution. Russia's allies recognized, almost immediately, the Provisional Government as the legitimate governing body of Russia and began to supply it generously with war credits.

The two most important issues facing the Provisional Government were agrarian discontent and the continuation of the war. Russia's peasants wanted land and they wanted it immediately. The Provisional Government, however, believed in acting with deliberation and according to the law. It refused to sanction peasant seizure of land despite the increasing disorder in the countryside. Instead, it appointed a commission to collect data on which future agrarian legislation was to be based. It was a decision that was inadequate to the emergency. As to the war, the members of the Provisional Government continued to honor the tsar's commitments to Russia's allies by participating in the fight against Germany and its allies. Most of the members hoped that Russia would win the war and gain the territories that had been promised to Russia.

The Provisional Government was also faced with the demands of the soviets and socialists. The soviets were councils consisting of deputies representing the people who had elected them. The soviet of Petrograd was formed in March 1917, but at the same time soviets were organized throughout Russia's military units, in factories, in workshops and in the rural areas. The soviets represented the more radical interests of the lower classes and were largely composed of socialists of various kinds.

The Socialist Revolutionaries were the most numerous of the socialist groups. They concerned themselves with the burdens of the peasants. They wished to establish peasant socialism by seizing the great landed estates and creating rural democracy. Since the beginning of the twentieth century, the Socialist Revolutionaries had come to rely on the use of political terrorism to accomplish their goals.

Since 1893, Russia also had a Marxist Social Democratic Labor Party. It was divided, in 1903, into two factions, the Mensheviks and Bolsheviks. The Mensheviks believed that Russian socialism would grow gradually and peacefully and that the tsar's government should be replaced by a democratic republic in which the socialists would cooperate with bourgeois political parties. Working under a democratic system, the socialists would gradually become the dominant political force and would organize a socialistic society through parliamentary means. They would not resort to crime or undemocratic methods to attain their goals. The Bolsheviks, the other faction, advocated the establishment of socialism through revolution. This faction had come under the leadership of Vladimir Ilyich Ulyanov who would become better known by his underground alias, Vladimir Lenin.

Lenin was born into a middle-class family in 1870. He received a legal education and became a lawyer. In 1887, he became a dedicated enemy of tsarism when his older brother was executed for participating in a plot to assassinate the tsar. Lenin's search for a revolutionary faith led him to Marxism and in 1894 he moved to St. Petersburg where he organized an illegal group known as the Union for the Liberation of the Working Class. Arrested for his activities, Lenin was sent as a political prisoner to Siberia. After his release in 1900, he chose to go into exile in western Europe and eventually assumed the leadership of the Bolshevik faction of the Russian Social Democratic Labor Party.

Under Lenin's direction, the Bolsheviks became a party dedicated to revolution. Lenin believed that only a violent revolution could destroy a capitalist system and the revolt must be carried out under the leadership of a small party of well-disciplined professional revolutionaries. Between 1900 and 1917, Lenin spent most of his time in Switzerland. There he lived a lonely existence and developed his theoretical view of the special role a militant party should play in a country that, like Russia, was just achieving modern capitalism. The party, he argued, could achieve its aims only by recognizing the revolutionary potential in the peasants' desire for land. Lenin hoped one day to return to Russia to recruit the peasants in a revolution that would establish a socialist state patterned on Marxist ideology.

When the Provisional Government was formed in March 1917, Lenin believed the opportunity for the Bolsheviks to seize power in Russia had come. In April 1917, the German High Command, calculating that Lenin's agitation would disrupt and undermine Russia's war efforts, arranged to transport him in a sealed train through Germany to the Baltic Sea coastline. From there he could be brought by ferry to Finland. Lenin, his wife and several trusted colleagues eventually arrived in Russia by way of Finland. Shortly after their arrival, they were joined by other Marxists that the tsarist government had formerly imprisoned or who had been forced to flee abroad.

In a series of proposals known as his "April Theses," issued on April 20, 1917, Lenin presented a blueprint for revolutionary action. In the "April Theses," Lenin maintained that the soviets elected by soldiers, workers and peasants were ready made instruments of power. The Bolsheviks must work to gain control of these groups and then use them to overthrow the Provisional Government. At the same time, Bolshevik propaganda must seek mass support through a list of promises directed to the needs of the people: an end to the war; the redistribution of all land to the peasants; the transfer of factories and industries from capitalists to committees of workers; and the relegation of political power from the Provisional Government to the soviets. Three simple slogans summed up the Bolshevik program: "Peace, Land, Bread," "Workers Control of Production" and "All Power to the Soviets."

In late spring and early summer, the Provisional Government struggled to maintain control of Russia. The Provisional Government promised that a constituent assembly, called for in the fall of 1917, would confiscate and redistribute royal and monastic lands. The promise was meaningless since many peasants had already started, in March, to seize and divide up the estates of Russia's large landowners. People in the cities, suffering from rising inflation and dwindling food supplies, were becoming more discontented. Disorder in the factories rose as workers, demanding higher wages, organized strikes and participated in industrial sabotage.

The military situation was also deteriorating. The Petrograd soviet had issued its Army Order No. 1 in March to all Russian military forces encouraging them to remove their officers and to replace them with committees composed of "elected representatives of the lower ranks" of the army. Army Order No. 1 ended the government's control over the army and it led to the collapse of all military discipline. When the Provisional Government attempted to initiate a new military offensive against the Germans in July, the army simply dissolved. Masses of peasant soldiers, hungry, ragged and disgruntled, deserted their units and returned home to their native villages to join their families in seizing lands.

At the same time, the influence of the Bolsheviks in Russia continued to grow. By the end of October, the Bolsheviks were the majority in the Petrograd and Moscow soviets. The number of Bolshevik members had increased from 50,000 to 240,000. Meanwhile, reports of unrest abroad convinced Lenin that the world was on the threshold of a proletarian revolution and he decided that the time had come to overthrow the Provisional Government. Although he faced opposition within the Bolshevik ranks, he managed to gain support for his decision. He was especially fortunate to have the close cooperation of Leon Trotsky.

The Bolshevik takeover of political rule in Russia came relatively easy. Lenin and Trotsky organized a Military Revolutionary Committee within the Petrograd soviet to plot the overthrow of the government. Beginning on November 4, large demonstrations and mass meetings were addressed by Trotsky. On the evening of November 6, Bolshevik forces seized railroad and communication centers, post offices, electric power plants and other key places in Petrograd. At noon the next day they stormed the Winter Palace, the headquarters of the Provisional Government, and arrested or put to flight all the government's cabinet members. The Provisional Government had fallen almost without resistance. In less than a day, the Bolsheviks had carried out successfully their political revolution.

On the afternoon of November 7, Lenin announced to the National Congress of Soviets in Petrograd that he was transferring the political sovereignty of the Provisional Government to that body. The National Congress of Soviets represented the local soviets from all over the country. Lenin then maneuvered the National Congress of Soviets to accept the Council of Peoples' Commissars as the executive body of the new government. The Bolsheviks occupied the top positions in the Council of Peoples' Commissars. Lenin held the post of chairman and Trotsky was placed in charge of foreign affairs. Lenin pledged to build a socialist state and to end Russia's war with Germany.

In the first months, the Bolsheviks built the rudiments of a new order. Lenin nationalized all landowner estates and turned them over to local rural soviets. The action legitimized the peasants' previous seizure of land and assured the Bolsheviks of peasant support. Lenin also met the demands of urban workers by turning over the control of mines and factories to committees of workers. All imperial institutions were dismantled and all social titles and military ranks were abolished. A campaign was also initiated against the Russian Orthodox Church, an institution the Bolsheviks regarded as an ally of the tsar and an enemy of socialism. The church hierarchy was dismantled and its lands, buildings, utensils and vestments were nationalized. The debts incurred by the tsarist government were repudiated, a decision that angered the foreign governments that had provided funds to Russia before and during the war.

Confident that the majority of Russia's people favored their policies, the Bolsheviks allowed elections, by universal male suffrage, for a constituent assembly to be held. However, they were shocked when they learned that they polled about a quarter of the vote while their main adversaries, the Socialist Revolutionaries, polled more than sixty percent. The delegates elected to the constituent assembly met only once, on January 18, 1918. On the following day Lenin dissolved it by decree and sent guards bearing rifles to prevent it from ever meeting again. The anti-Bolshevik majority in the constituent assembly was furious at Lenin's act of pure force against the popular will, but there was no public outburst and the delegates disbanded.

One of Lenin's primary goals was to end Russia's war against Germany. He started peace negotiations with the Germans in December 1917. The Germans, aware of Russia's helplessness, demanded among other things, Finland, the Ukraine, eastern Poland and the Baltic provinces. If Germany's demands were met, Russia would lose more than a million square kilometers of territory, which included a third of its arable land, a quarter of its population and three-quarters of its deposits of iron and coal. Lenin balked at Germany's demands but, with the German military advancing into Russia and the Russian army disintegrating, he believed that he had no other option but to agree to the demands. The treaty that took Russia out of the war was signed at Brest-Litovsk on March 3, 1918. Nine days later, Lenin moved his government to Moscow, the center of Russia.

After the signing of the Treaty of Brest-Litovsk, Russia plunged into a civil war. Throughout Russia, there emerged groups that were hostile to the Bolsheviks who now called themselves the Russian Communist Party. Lenin changed the name of his party in 1918 because the word communist implied a concern for the human community. The counterrevolutionaries, collectively called "Whites," were led by former tsarist military officers and included members of the outlawed nobility, former landowners, supporters of the tsar and socialists from rival parties, including the Mensheviks and Socialist Revolutionaries. By late June 1918, Russia's allies of World War One intervened in the Russian Civil War on behalf of the opponents of the Communists. The Japanese occupied Russia's far eastern provinces, while the French, the Americans and the British sent supplies as well as troops to aid the White forces. The Allies were eager to see the Whites win the Russian Civil War, not only to prevent the spread of communism but also because they hoped that under different political leadership Russia would reenter the war against Germany.

To meet the new danger, the Communists hastily formed the Red Army in the summer of 1918. Under the leadership of Leon Trotsky, the appointed Commissar of War, the Red Army became a well-organized formidable fighting force. Trotsky reinstated the draft and even recruited and gave commands to former tsarist army officers. He insisted on rigid discipline. Soldiers who deserted or refused to obey orders were executed.

Between 1918 and 1921, the Red Army was forced to fight on many fronts. The first serious threat to the communist regime came from Siberia where a White army under Admiral Alexander Kolchak pushed westward and advanced almost to the Volga River before being stopped. Attacks also came from the Ukraine in the southeast and from the Baltic regions. In mid-1919, White forces under General Anton Denikin swept through the Ukraine and advanced almost to Moscow, Lenin's new capital city. At one point, in late 1919, three separate White armies were closing in on the Communists. They were eventually pushed back and by 1920 the major White forces had been defeated and the Ukraine had been retaken. The next year, the communist regime regained control over the independent nationalist governments in the Caucasus: Georgia, Russian Armenia and Azerbaijan.

The Communists were equally successful in crushing political opposition in the territories under their control. Following a failed assassination attempt on Lenin, the Communists initiated a Red Terror campaign. It was conducted by Felix Dzerzhinsky, the chief of a newly organized secret police force which was titled the All-Russian Extraordinary Commission for the Struggle Against Counterrevolution and Sabotage. Known by its acronym of Cheka, its agents arrested, tried and executed anyone who was known to be or who was suspected of being hostile to the Communists. The place of enemies (enemies of the people), in Lenin's words, was "against the wall." Cheka killed as many as two hundred thousand opponents of the regime. The most famous victims were Tsar Nicholas II and his family who were executed in Ekaterinburg in July 1918. To prevent organized opposition, Lenin's government outlawed all political parties except the Russian Communist Party and thereby he converted Russia into a one-party dictatorship.

During the Russian Civil War, Lenin instituted a policy known as War Communism. It was introduced in 1918 to deal with the plummeting agricultural and industrial production,with soaring inflation and with rising hunger in the cities. Under War Communism the government nationalized transportation and communication facilities as well as banks, mines, factories and businesses that employed more than ten workers. The land holdings of poor peasants were exempted from confiscation, but the Communists did seize grain from the peasants to feed the people in the cities and the soldiers in the Red Army. The peasants were left with only a bare minimum for subsistence.

Socializing the Russian economy would help the Communists win the Russian Civil War but it would also bring the country to the brink of collapse. The government's program of requisitioning food so alienated the peasants that many grew only enough food for their immediate needs. Added to this development was a drought which caused a great famine between 1920 and 1922; it claimed the lives of as many as five million people. The socialization of the economy brought chaos to Russia's industries and mines as well. Many workers appointed to managerial positions lacked experience and this caused industrial output to fall. By 1921, the output was only 21 percent of the 1918 level. Many industrial workers moved from the cities to the rural areas in search of employment. Transportation systems broke down and Russia's exports shrank to a fraction of the 1917 level.

Lenin made an ideological retreat to prevent the collapse of Communist Russia. In March 1921, he adopted the New Economic Policy, also known by its initials as NEP, which was a compromise between socialist and free enterprise practices. Lenin described it as "a step backwards in order to take two steps forward," a temporary measure that would be abandoned as soon as the economy was stabilized. Under the New Economic Policy, the State retained control over large industries, mines, banking, transportation and communication facilities and foreign trade. It did, however, permit private local trade and it restored small shops and factories (those with fewer than twenty workers) to their former owners. Under the New Economic Policy, a peasant still had to pay a governmental tax which was a fixed portion of his crop yield but he was allowed to sell the remainder of his crop to the State if he wished or to a private purchaser if he preferred. Within limits, a peasant was permitted to lease additional land and hire labor. Peasant agriculture became capitalist once again and the profit motive was brought back. Concessions were also made to foreign entrepreneurs who wanted to exploit the mines and oil wells in Russia.

In December 1922, the Union of Soviet Socialist Republics was formally established. Commonly called the Soviet Union, it was a federal union consisting of territories, regions, nominally autonomous states and republics. Of the four republics, the Russian Soviet Federated Socialist Republic (Russia) was the largest and the most influential. The other three were the Transcaucasian Soviet Federated Socialist Republic (Armenia, Azerbaijan and Georgia), the Ukrainian Soviet Socialist Republic (Ukraine) and the Belorussian Soviet Socialist Republic (Belorussia). As time went on, the boundaries of the republics would shift and the number of republics would increase.

The Communists would formalize their authoritarian rule in a constitution drafted in 1924. The constitution granted the franchise to all productive workers over the age of eighteen but not to the bourgeoisie or to those closely identified with tsarism and the Russian Orthodox Church. The Party leadership demonstrated their distrust of the Russian peasants by making each urban vote of the electorate equivalent to five rural votes. Ostensibly, political power rested with the elected local soviets (councils or cells) that were organized according to occupation. These soviets elected delegates to the Congress of Soviets of their canton, the smallest administrative unit, and each of the congresses in turn sent delegates to a congress at the next administrative level. The All-Union Congress of Soviets was the culmination of the elections and it was to meet every two years. Because the All-Union Congress of Soviets was not a permanent body, the members (delegates) of this body elected an executive committee to act on their behalf between sessions. The executive committee was called the Central Executive Committee.

The Central Executive Committee was to meet three times a year. During the interval between the sessions of the Central Executive Committee, the Presidium of the Committee supervised the government administration. Finally, the Central Executive Committee elected the Council of People's Commissars, which served as the executive arm of the government. The members of the Council of People's Commissars were elected for a two-year term. The Council was commonly called Sovnarkom which is an abbreviation for Soviet Narodnykh Kommissarov (Council of People's Commissars).

The constitution did not mention the Russian Communist Party but the Party was the real center of political power. The central Party institutions included the Party Congress, the Central Committee, the Politburo (political bureau), the Secretariat and the Party commissions. The Party Congress was expected to convene every year for about a week. It was attended by delegates who had been elected by republic Party congresses or by conferences of territories, provinces and autonomous republics. While in session, the Party Congress voted on several kinds of issues and all decisions were unanimous.

Most important, the Party Congress formally elected the members of the Central Committee which was authorized to govern the Party until the next Party Congress. Because the Central Committee was too large and cumbersome to perform its duties, it delegated its authority to the Politburo.

The original Politburo was established two weeks before the Bolsheviks came to power in 1917. It was formed as a means to centralize decision making. Since the Bolshevik Revolution, it consisted of the highest Party and government officials in the Soviet Union. The Politburo was composed of full (voting) members and of candidate (non-voting) members. In 1922 the Politburo was made up of seven full (voting) members: Vladimir Lenin, Leon Trotsky, Joseph Stalin, Grigory Zinoviev, Lev Kamenev, Alexie Rykov and Mikhail Tomsky. The three candidate (non-voting) members were Nikolai Bukharin, Mikhail Kalinin and Vyacheslav Molotov. The Politburo was the highest political decision-making body in the Soviet Union. It made all the major policy decisions for both the Party and the government.

Lenin's health began to deteriorate after Dora Kaplan, in an attempt to assassinate him, shot him in 1918. Severe headaches limited his sleep and he began to suffer from fatigue. Lenin decided he needed someone to assist him in controlling the Russian Communist Party. At the Party Conference held in April 1922, Lenin suggested that a new post within the government should be created. The man who was chosen for this post was Joseph Stalin. He was assigned to the position of General Secretary.

# Chapter 1

# Stalin's Rise to Power

Born Joseph Djugashvili in 1879 in the Georgian region of Transcaucasia, Stalin was the son of a poor shoemaker. Admitted to a seminary to be trained for the priesthood, young Stalin was later expelled for holding radical opinions. He joined the Bolsheviks in 1903 and came to Vladimir Lenin's attention after staging a daring bank robbery to obtain funds for the Bolshevik cause. In 1912, Lenin made Stalin a member of the Bolshevik's Central Committee and in that same year told him to write a work on Marxism and nationalism, which Stalin completed to Lenin's satisfaction. In 1917, Stalin arrived in Petrograd about three weeks before Lenin's arrival and worked as editor of the Bolshevik paper, *Pravda*. In 1922, he became General Secretary of the Russian Communist Party's Central Committee. As General Secretary, Stalin prepared the agenda for the Politburo meetings; he supplied the documentation for points under debate and passed the decisions made by the Politburo down to the lower levels in the Russian Communist Party.

Soon after Stalin's appointment to General Secretary, Lenin went into a hospital to have a bullet removed from his body; it had been there since Dora Kaplan's assassination attempt. It was hoped that this surgery would restore his health. That, however, would not be the case. Soon afterwards, a blood vessel broke in Lenin's brain. It left Lenin paralyzed down his right side and for some time he was unable to speak. As Lenin's assistant, Stalin had suddenly become very important.

While Lenin was immobilized, Stalin made full use of his powers as General Secretary. At the Party Congress, he had been granted permission to expel unsatisfactory Party members. As General Secretary, Stalin also had the authority to remove people from and to appoint people to important positions in the government. The new holders of government posts were fully aware that they owed their positions to Stalin. They also knew that if their behavior did not please Stalin, they would be replaced.

Surrounded by his supporters, Stalin's confidence began to grow. In October 1922, he disagreed with Lenin over the issue of foreign trade. When the matter was discussed by the Party's Central Committee, Stalin's policy rather than Lenin's was accepted. Fearing that Stalin was taking over the leadership of the Party, Lenin wrote Leon Trotsky and asked for his support. Trotsky agreed and at the next meeting of the Party's Central Committee the decision on foreign trade was reversed. Lenin, who was too ill to attend the meeting, wrote to Trotsky congratulating him on his success and suggested that in the future they should work together against Stalin.

Stalin learned about the contents of Lenin's letter to Trotsky from his (Stalin's) wife, Nadezhda Alliluyeva, who worked in Lenin's private office. Stalin was furious. He believed that should Lenin and Trotsky work together against him, his political career would come to an end. In a fit of temper, Stalin made an abusive telephone call to Lenin's wife, Nadezhda Krupskaya, accusing her of endangering Lenin's life by allowing him to write letters while he was so ill.

After Nadezhda told her husband of the phone call, Lenin decided that Stalin must not succeed him as the leader of the Party. Lenin knew that he was close to death, so he dictated to his secretary a letter that he wanted to serve as his last will and testament. He wrote:

> Having become General Secretary, comrade Stalin has concentrated immeasurable power in his hands and I am not sure that he will always know how to use that power with sufficient caution. . . . On the other hand, Comrade Trotsky . . . has distinguished himself not only by his outstanding abilities. . . . He is certainly the ablest man on the present Committee, but is possessed of excessive self-confidence and has a disposition to be too much attracted by the purely administrative aspect of affairs. . . . These characteristics of the two most eminent leaders of the present Central Committee may, unintentionally, lead to a split in the Party if the Party does not take measures to prevent it. . . . [1]

On the fourth of January 1923, Lenin added a postscript to his earlier will and testament:

> Stalin is too rude, and this fault . . . becomes intolerable in the office of General Secretary. . . . I invite the comrades to consider ways of removing Stalin from this post and appointing somebody who is better in all respects than Stalin, namely one more tolerant, more loyal, more polite, more considerate towards his comrades, less capricious, etc.[2]

Three days after writing the above will and testament, Lenin suffered a third stroke. Lenin was no longer able to speak or write. Although he lived for another ten months, he ceased to exist as a political power within the Soviet Union. It was assumed that Trotsky would replace Lenin as the leader of the Russian Communist Party.

To prevent Trotsky's rise to leadership, Stalin established a triumvirate composed of himself and two "old Bolsheviks," Grigory Zinoviev and Lev Kamenev. The latter two men had joined the Russian Social Democratic Labor Party in 1901. Both joined Lenin's faction, the Bolsheviks, within the party in 1903 and both were with Lenin in Petrograd at the time of the Bolshevik Revolution in 1917. By 1921 Zinoviev had become the head of the Petrograd Party organization, the chairman of the Petrograd Soviet and a member of the Politburo of the Russian Communist Party. He was also the chairman of the executive committee of the Communist International (Comintern). Kamenev became a member of the Politburo in 1919 and was chairman of the Moscow Soviet.

Isaac Deutscher, the author of *Stalin* published in 1949, pointed out:

> What made for the solidarity of the three men was their determination to prevent Trotsky from succeeding to the leadership of the party [Party]. Separately, neither could measure up to Trotsky. Jointly, they represented a powerful combination of talent and influence. Zinoviev was the politician, the orator, the demagogue with popular appeal. Kamenev was the strategist of the group, its solid brain, trained in matters of doctrine, which were to play a paramount part in the contest for power. Stalin was the tactician of the triumvirate and its organizing force. Between them, the three men virtually controlled the whole party [Party], through it, the Government.[3]

Trotsky and his supporters, together known as the Left Opposition, criticized Stalin and his allies. They accused them of turning the Party into a dictatorship. They demanded a restoration of Party democracy. Trotsky expressed his concern on the fifth of December 1923, in a published open letter in which he called for more debate in the Party concerning the way the country was being governed. He argued that Party members should exercise their right to criticize "without fear." He further argued that the first people who needed to be removed from the Party were "those who at the first voice of criticism or objection or protest are inclined to demand one's party [Party] ticket for the purpose of repression." Trotsky went on to suggest that anyone who "dares to terrorize members in the party [Party]" should be expelled from the Party.[4]

Zinoviev was furious with Trotsky for making the above comments and proposed that Trotsky be arrested immediately. Stalin, aware of Trotsky's immense popularity, opposed the move as being too dangerous. He did, however, encourage Zinoviev and Kamenev to attack Trotsky.

Stalin waited until the end of December 1923, before addressing the issue of Party democracy raised by Trotsky and the Left Opposition. Stalin did not believe that the Party was a debating society. Debate, he argued, would lead to the creation of factions and groupings within the Party. Without mentioning Trotsky, Stalin asked the question: "Did the opposition [Trotsky and his supporters] demand that Lenin's rules, which banned factions and groupings inside the party [Party], should be abolished?"[5]

Lenin died on January 21, 1924, and following his death there emerged the cult of Lenin. Inspired by genuine reverence for Lenin and by a political desire to move the masses around a potent symbol, the members of the Politburo had Lenin's body embalmed and placed in a sarcophagus inside a mausoleum for public viewing. The mausoleum, designed as a cube-like structure and made of red granite, was built on Red Square in front of the Kremlin Wall in Moscow. Outside of the mausoleum, a large number of people daily would stand in line for hours to enter and view the mummified body of Lenin. The writings of Lenin became sacred and irrefutable. Images of the father of the Soviet Union appeared everywhere in stone, in metal, on canvas and in print. Lenin corners, analogous to the icon corners of Russian Orthodoxy, became fixtures in nearly every institution and Lenin's name graced thousands of libraries, educational institutions and streets. On January 25, 1924, just five days after Lenin's death, Petrograd, originally named St. Petersburg, was renamed Leningrad, meaning Lenin's City.

Trotsky's main hope of succeeding Lenin as leader of the Russian Communist Party was for Lenin's last will and testament to be published. In May 1924, Lenin's widow, Nadezhda Krupskaya, demanded that the Central Committee of the Party reveal to the rest of the Party the contents of her husband's will and testament. Zinoviev argued strongly against its publication. He finished his speech with the words: "You have all witnessed our harmonious cooperation in the last few months; and, like myself, you will be happy to say that Lenin's fears have proved baseless."[6] The new members of the Party's Central Committee, who had been sponsored by Stalin, decided that Lenin's will and testament was not to be made public.

On November 19 of 1924, Stalin felt strong enough to denounce Trotsky directly and publicly in a speech that he made to the plenum (a full assembly) of the Communist group in the All-Union Central Council of Trade Unions (A.U.C.C.T.U.). In the speech, Stalin defined what he labeled Trotskyism and he explained how it differed from Leninism.

Seven days later, on November 26, 1924, Stalin's speech titled "Trotskyism or Leninism?" was published in *Pravda.*

In January 1925, the triumvirate was able to force Trotsky to resign as People's Commissar of Army and Navy Affairs and as Chairman of the Revolutionary Military Council. Some of Trotsky's supporters pleaded with him to organize a military coup d'état but Trotsky rejected the idea. Deutscher, the author of *Stalin* (1949) maintained: "He left office without the slightest attempt at rallying in his defense the army [Red Army] he had created and led for seven years. He still regarded the party [Russian Communist Party], no matter how or by whom it was led, as the legitimate spokesman of the working class."[7]

The year 1925 proved to be an unusual year for Trotsky. After losing his Red Army and Navy Affairs posts, he was effectively unemployed throughout the winter and spring. In May he was given three posts: chairman of the Concessions Committee, head of the Electro-technical Board and chairman of the Scientific-technical Board of Industry. Later in the year, Trotsky resigned from his two technical positions and concentrated on his work in the Concessions Committee.

In the meantime, Kamenev and Zinoviev had broken with Stalin over issues such as building "socialism in one country." It was a thesis formulated by Nikolai Bukharin, the leading Party theoretician and editor of *Pravda*. Bukharin argued that socialism could be developed in a single country, even in one as underdeveloped as Russia. Bukharin stated that revolution need not be encouraged in the world's capitalist countries since Russia could and should achieve socialism alone. "Socialism in one country" was adopted by Stalin and it became a hall mark of Stalinism.

What Stalin told the Party was this:

> Of course we are looking forward to international revolution. Of course, we have been brought up in the school of Marxism; and we know that contemporary social and political struggles are, by their very nature, international. Of course, we still believe the victory of the proletariat in the west to be near; and we are bound in honor to do what we can to speed it up. But . . . do not worry so much about all that international revolution. Even if it were to be delayed indefinitely, even if it were never to occur, we in this country [the Soviet Russia] are capable of developing into a fully-fledged, classless society. Let us then concentrate on our great constructive task. Those who tell you that this is utopia, that I am preaching national narrow-mindedness, are themselves either adventurers or pusillanimous Social Democrats. We . . . have already done more for socialism than the proletariat of all other countries taken together; and, left alone . . . we shall do the rest of the job.[8]

How can a country like Russia achieve socialism? Stalin pointed to Russia's great assets, her vast spaces and enormous riches in raw materials. A proletarian government could, in his view, through its control of industry and credit, develop those resources and carry the building of socialism to a successful conclusion. It would be supported in this endeavor by the vast majority of people which would include the peasants. Stalin's answer to the question was clear and positive. "We," he asserted, "are able to stand on our own feet, to build and to complete the building of socialism."[9]

After Kamenev and Zinoviev broke away from Stalin, they formed what was called the New Opposition. However, they were defeated quickly by Stalin. The latter was supported by Bukharin and Alexie Rykov at the Fourteenth Party Congress held in December 1925. Rykov was the deputy chairman of the Council of People's Commissars also known as Sovnarkom.

Following their defeat, Kamenev and Zinoviev, in an attempt to subvert Stalin's growing influence, joined Trotsky and his Left Opposition in what became known as the United Opposition. But by 1926 it was already too late to mount a strong challenge to Stalin's growing power. Through skillful maneuvering, Stalin had been able increasingly to secure control over the Party apparatus, eroding what little power the oppositionists had.

In October 1926, Trotsky was removed from the Politburo. A year later, again in October, Trotsky and Zinoviev were removed from the Central Committee of the Party. On November 15, 1927, it was announced that Trotsky and Zinoviev were purged from the Party and in the following month the Fifteenth Party Congress declared that Trotskyist views and the Left Opposition were incompatible with Party membership. Thereafter, all leading oppositionists, including Kamenev, were expelled from the Party.

After their expulsion by the Fifteenth Party Congress, Kamenev, Zinoviev and their supporters surrendered to Stalin "admitting their mistakes" and renouncing their alliance with Trotsky and the Left Opposition. They were readmitted to the Russian Communist Party in 1928. Trotsky and most of his followers, on the other hand, refused to bow to Stalin and were exiled to Siberia and Central Asia. Trotsky was exiled to Alma Ata in January 1928.

A year later, on January 20, 1929, Trotsky was informed that he was to be expelled from the Soviet Union. The decision was communicated to him by GPU agents as follows: "Considered: the case of Citizen Trotsky, Leon Davidovich, under Article 58/10 of the Criminal Code [also known as the Penal Code] on a charge of counter-revolutionary activity expressing itself in the organization of an illegal anti-Soviet party, whose activity has lately been directed toward provoking anti-Soviet actions and preparing for an armed struggle against the Soviet power. (see Document One) Resolved: Citizen Trotsky, Leon Davidovich, to be deported from the territory of the U.S.S.R." Trotsky, his wife Natalia Sedova and his son Lyova (Leon Sedov was his full adult name) were exiled from the Soviet Union.[10]

## NOTES

1. Victor Serge and Natalia Sedova Trotsky, *The Life and Death of Leon Trotsky*, 113.

2. Serge and Trotsky, *The Life and Death of Leon Trotsky*, 114.

3. Isaac Deutscher, *Stalin: A Political Biography* (Oxford, England: Oxford University Press, 1949), 255.

4. Deutscher, *Stalin: A Political Biography*, 264.

5. Deutscher, *Stalin: A Political Biography*, 265.

6. Deutscher, *Stalin: A Political Biography*, 272.

7. Pravda, November 26, 1924.

8. Deutscher, *Stalin: A Political Biography*, 297.

9. Deutscher, *Stalin: A Political Biography*, 290.

10. Deutscher, *Stalin: A Political Biography*, 284–285.

# Chapter 2

# Nicolai Koral

## Collective Farm Worker

Stalin had won the struggle for power within the Russian Communist Party and as the leader of the Party he would use that position to transform the Soviet Union into a totalitarian socialist state. Lenin had been forced to retreat from socializing the Russian economy because of the chaos that had been brought on by the Russian Civil War. He had instituted the New Economic Policy and through it had succeeded in rescuing Russia from an economic crisis. But the crisis was past and Stalin, who remained committed to the Communist dream, now wanted to remove from the Soviet Union all forms of capitalism. He began the process in 1928 by ending the New Economic Policy and launching the first of several five-year plans. The First Five-year Plan marked the beginning of Stalinism.

The goals of the First Five-year Plan were to increase agricultural production through mechanized collective farming and to develop large-scale industries that were to be owned and managed by the State (Stalin and the Russian Communist Party). The implementation of the first goal would begin after the Kulaks, through their actions, created food shortages. Under the New Economic Policy, private ownership and free enterprise had been permitted to flourish in the countryside in order to ensure enough food for the workers living in the cities. Many land-owning farmers had become so prosperous that they had the means to hire labor and lend money to others within their villages. The Russian Communist Party called them Kulaks, an old derisive term used to describe grasping merchants and usurers. During the months of 1928 and 1929, the Kulaks and other farmers withheld their grain from the marketplace because agricultural prices were too low. Food shortages occurred in the cities which caused potential unrest. Sometime during these difficult months, Stalin decided that agriculture needed to be collectivized in order to produce sufficient grain for food and for export and to free peasants for labor in newly constructed factories.

21

In late 1929, Stalin declared that the Kulaks, as a social class, were to be eliminated. He accused them of trying to sabotage the State by withholding grain and threatening the cities with famine. Stalin's actions against the Kulaks were part of the State's plan to erase private ownership of land and to collectivize farming. The Kulaks probably numbered less than five percent of the rural population but in time a Kulak was identified as any peasant who opposed collectivization. Party agents were sent into the countryside to expropriate the land, the farming equipment and the livestock owned by the Kulaks. The victims were then rounded up and deported to prison labor camps or exiled to desolate regions in Siberia. Perhaps some 2,000,000 households, as many as 10,000,000 people, suffered the fate of deportation or exile.

Peasants who were not expropriated were pressured to become members of newly created collective farms. Joining a collective farm meant that a peasant family was required to give up their land, their farming equipment and all their livestock except for one milk cow, geese and chickens. Most land-owning peasants cherished their lands and wanted no part of collectivization. In desperate revolt, many burned their crops, smashed their equipment, and killed and ate their livestock rather than turn their possessions over to the State. More than half of the horses in the Soviet Union, forty-five percent of the cattle and two-thirds of the sheep and goats were slaughtered. Millions of peasants left the land and moved to the cities; their lands lay uncultivated. It resulted in a famine which over a four-year period would kill millions of people in the Soviet Union.

The peasant resistance persuaded Stalin, in March 1930, to call a brief halt to collectivization. He justified the slow down in an article titled *"Dizzy with Success."* In it he blamed the consequences of collectivization on local Party officials who had been too eager to rush through the process, contradicting his own order of a few months before. Thus, Stalin managed to escape some of the hatred that would otherwise have been directed against him.

The State soon resumed its collectivization program and by the end of the first year of the First Five-year Plan about fifty percent of the farms in the Soviet Union had been collectivized. An additional ten percent were collectivized during the next three years so that by 1933, sixty percent of the farms were collectivized. The number would continue to rise and by 1939 more than ninety-six percent of the farms in the Soviet Union were collectivized. In 1941, there were some 250,000 agricultural collectives that supported some 19,000,000 families.

A collective farm (kolkhoz) was a community of farmers in a designated area that included a store, a school, a library, a hospital and a clubhouse. It was created by combining a large number of small farms into one large farm. The average size of a collective farm was 5,900 hectares (14,673 acres). The land used by the farm belonged to the State and it was leased to the collective in perpetuity. Theoretically, it was a self-financed cooperative venture carried out by its members, but in fact it was governed by the State's regulations, a rural soviet and district Party officials. The members of a collective elected the farm's managing committee and a chairman. The farm chairman was usually a Party member and he was nominated by the Party. It was the chairman who oversaw the production of goods which was to meet the production goals determined by the State's planning boards. He was also expected to provide ideological leadership for the members of the farm. A chairman that did not meet the ideological purity requirements, was removed.

The income of a collective farm member was determined by the number of workday credits that she or he earned. Work performed, rather than hours expended, was the basis for awarding credits. A tractor driver, for example, might earn three workday credits for plowing a hectare (two- and one-half acres) of land in ten hours, but a less skilled farm hand, weeding a vegetable patch, might receive only one workday credit for the same number of hours of work. The workday credits for each farm member were added up at the end of the fiscal year but the distribution of money and produce was made to each member after the collective farm's debts had been paid and after certain obligations had been satisfied. The collective farm was required to pay taxes to the State. The farm's leadership also had to set aside funds that would be needed to rent machinery, buy livestock, construct buildings, purchase seed and provide the members of the farm with educational and cultural activities. If the year's harvest had been abundant, the members of the collective farm would live quite well. If the harvest had been poor, they would suffer.

The State assisted and controlled collective farms through the supply of heavy agricultural equipment furnished by a Machine Tractor Station (MTS). Collective farms were not permitted to have their own tractors or combines; they were required to rent them from a State-owned station located nearby. The collective farm paid the Machine Tractor Station for the use of the machines not in money but in produce and this produce went to the State since the Machine Tractor Station was owned by the State. Technicians at the station repaired, during the winter months, the machinery that was returned to the station following the harvest season. They were also at the service of a collective farm for advice regarding fertilizers, irrigation, crop rotation and other agricultural matters. Administrators of a Machine Tractor Station could affect the success of collective farms by deciding when and to whom to allot tractors and how many tractors to allot. The goodwill of the station administrators was of utmost importance to a collective farm.

During the Stalin years the collective farms were required to turn over a large percentage of their produce to the State. The State purchased the produce at fixed prices and the State set the prices. The State then charged higher prices when it sold the produce to the consumers in the towns and cities throughout the Soviet Union. Sometimes the price that was charged by the State for an agricultural product sold in a city store, which was also owned and managed by the State, was substantially higher than what a collective farm had received for it. The markup in price and the sale of exported produce helped the State finance the industrialization of the Soviet Union.

Stalin's collectivization campaign also included the creation of state farms. A state farm (sovkhoz) was quite distinct from a collective farm. The state farms were created through the confiscation by the State of large, landed estates and the average size of a state farm was 15,300 hectares (37,791 acres). A state farm was exclusively a State enterprise. It was given production goals and the operating budgets were determined by the State's planning agency. The entire output of the farm was delivered to the State's procurement agency. The state farm workers were employees of the State. They were paid a salary and were guaranteed a minimum wage. An employee of a state farm worked, as a rule, a forty-six-hour week and was paid overtime. There were no Machine Tractor Stations associated with state farms; each farm had its own mechanized agricultural equipment.

Each family in a collective farm and in a state farm was assigned a private plot of cultivable land. The plot, usually called a kitchen garden, was generally between one-fourth to one-half a hectare large (one to one and a quarter acre large). On this land, the family was entitled to grow vegetables for their own consumption and to raise livestock. A family was permitted to own one cow and two calves up to two years of age, one sow and a litter of pigs, ten sheep or goats and an unlimited number of poultry. The family was allowed to sell on the free market whatever they grew or raised on their private plot. A family was also permitted to own a dwelling place and minor implements and the entire homestead could be sold or left by will to the owner's descendants.

## NIKOLAI KORAL

Nikolai Koral was a member of a collective farm in the 1930s. During the Great Patriotic War (World War Two) he was brought to Germany, as a prisoner, to work on Germany's farms. Following the war, he was interviewed and asked to describe his life experiences as a member of a collective farm in the Soviet Union. In the following paragraphs, Nikolai recounts his experiences as a collective farm member:

Collectivization was started in our village in 1930. It began with the liquidation of the well-to-do peasants, the so-called Kulaks, within our district. First the government (the State) demanded that they [the village Kulaks] deliver to the State thirty-six hundred pounds of grain. After the demand was met, the government ordered them to send another eighteen hundred pounds of grain. A third demand was issued by the government but by this time most of the village Kulaks had nothing left. Consequently, a commission was sent to the village. They inventoried the properties of the Kulaks and brought each case to the district court. The court confiscated the possessions of the Kulaks and sentenced them to ten years of hard labor in some concentration camp. This is how the village Kulaks, as a class of people, were liquidated.

Peasants of average means were dealt with in a similar fashion. Those who refused to join a kolkhoz [collective farm] or who did not fulfill the government's demands were also taken to court. The penalty was often the confiscation of property, the eviction of the family and six to seven years in exile.

Through this kind of coercion, many peasants were gradually persuaded to join a collective. In 1930, some 30 to 40 per cent of the peasants entered the collectives. However, the Soviet [Russian] Communist Party demanded that all the peasants be collectivized. Thus, specially authorized government agents were sent from a regional collectivization headquarters into the villages. Through one means or another they made sure that the peasants entered a kolkhoz.

Many peasants, having been forcefully enlisted in a collective, did not want to work. If this became the case in a collective, the government would send in agents of the State's secret police as well as regional agents to determine who was guilty of instigating resistance. Often, innocent people were accused of spreading anti collectivization propaganda. These people would be arrested and exiled.

The pay rate in a collective farm was computed on the basis of workdays. A person's annual income was determined by the total number of workdays he or she had completed. The peasant was promised that at the end of the year he or she would receive ten to fifteen rubles in currency and twenty to twenty-five pounds of grain for each workday unit. In practice, this never happened. The individual rate was about one ruble in money and less than a pound of grain per workday unit. The grain that the peasant did receive was that which the government had rejected as low grade. In years of especially good harvest, the kolkhoznik [collective farmer] might receive up to ten pounds of grain per workday unit.

Before collectivization, the peasant worked his land with diligence and with great energy. He knew what he was working for and what he would earn for his labor. After collectivization, he was less sure of his return and worked only to make the day end faster. His greatest interest and devotion were to his own plot of land, his kitchen garden. According to Soviet law, each kolkhoznik was entitled to a piece of land. On this land he was permitted to grow anything he desired. Because the members of the collective farm had their kitchen gardens, they were able to stay alive.

Work in the fields of the kolkhoz consumed thirteen hours of a workday. I was one of those who worked the fields. I started work at 6:00 A.M. and worked until eight o'clock in the evening. I was given an hour off for supper. The workday unit was measured according to established norms. For example, the plowing of one and a half acres of land with two horses equaled one workday.

After the village was collectivized, the peasants began to treat the horses badly. Since the horses were no longer their personal property but belonged to the kolkhoz, they decided that there was no advantage in taking the time to treat them well. This was also true of the agricultural machinery. When a kolkhoznik was finished using a machine, he usually left without oiling it. He wanted to get home as soon as possible.

Our kolkhoz was poorly supplied. There were stores in the village but they were poorly supplied. Three or four suits [suits for men] would arrive on average each month. This was not enough to supply the thousands of collective farm members. When suits did arrive, the peasants never saw them because they were taken by the chairman of the village Soviet and by other Party members in the local administration.

About all that the average kolkhoznik could hope for from time to time were two to three yards of cotton material. Most of the peasants wore clothes that were made in the home. If a person was able to get hold of some leather, he could try to make for himself a pair of boots. However, much of the footwear was nothing more than rags that were tied around the feet. During the summer season, most of the peasants went barefooted.

Even the necessities were scarce. Salt, matches and dishes were not available in our village store. Sometimes, earthenware made by peasants was brought in but there was never enough to meet the need.

In 1933 our village was struck by a famine. The harvest had been abundant in the kolkhoz but the government took everything from us. Even the food that was produced in our kitchen gardens had to be handed over to the government. Throughout the hunger period that year (1933) we ate dead horses, grass and weeds. At the beginning of collectivization, our village had three thousand people; after the man-made famine, eighteen hundred people were left. The same was true of all the surrounding villages that had been turned into collective farms.

Before the Bolshevik Revolution, I had twenty-seven acres of land and I lived well. Collectivization took my land, my barn, my horses and my farming equipment. I was permitted to keep a two-room hut [house] and a shed. Before the Bolshevik Revolution, I sold on the open market yearly some three thousand to four thousand pounds of grain. I also sold pigs and calves. When I became a member of the kolkhoz, all of this was taken from me.

The theft of kolkhoz property by a kolkhoznik a [a member of a collective farm] could lead to severe punishment. Under a law passed in 1932, a person found guilty of theft could be sentenced to prison for ten years. One of my neighbors was sentenced for seven years for tearing off a handful of wheat while he was on his way home from the fields.

There was a special building in the village that was used for meetings at which various issues concerning our kolkhoz were discussed. During the discussions those who were in attendance were expected by the kolkhoz chairman to express only opinions that were acceptable to the Party organization. If anyone spoke in opposition to something proposed by the Party administration, he was likely to receive a prison term of up to three to five years and was labeled an "enemy of the people." This happened to a kolkhoznik at one of the meetings in 1934. At the meeting it was suggested that discipline be tightened within the collective. One peasant [kolkhoznik] objected to the proposed suggestion saying that tightening discipline would not remedy a single problem. "Anyway," he added, "the whole thing is just deceit. We strengthened our discipline but received nothing in return." For these words, he was sentenced to prison for five years.

Before the Bolshevik Revolution, we had a church that almost everyone attended on days of worship. During collectivization, the church building was closed and it was desecrated. Only the memory of past worship services remained and religious holidays were celebrated secretly.

One day, a detachment of men sent by the government arrived in the village while the priest was conducting a religious service. The priest continued the service and said that he would not leave the church before he was finished. When the service was completed, the government agents tried to arrest the priest. But the worshipers intervened. Shots were fired and a battle ensued. Fifteen peasants were killed and some fifty were arrested and taken away. We never heard from them again. The priest became ill and within three days he died.

A special brigade of men was organized and it went from house to house collecting Russian Orthodox icons. (see Glossary—icon) There were peasants who hid their icons and they would pray to them in secret. Every peasant had to sign a statement that he or she had given up his or her icon. Later, when the hidden icons were discovered, the owners were arrested and sentenced to a year of hard labor in a special work camp.

No steps were taken by the authorities to improve the living conditions in the village after it was collectivized. We had no electricity. Every few years we were promised that electricity would be brought into the village but it never came. We had no radios. There was a movie theater in the district center [a nearby town] but we had no time to go there. We were required to work on most Sundays and on the days that the government had identified as days of celebration. I never left the village. I never went to the district center or to any other town. If anyone had the desire to leave the kolkhoz, he would need the permission of the authorities.

The women in the kolkhoz had the same rights and duties as the men. In order to free the women for work, a village nursery was organized. A mother took her children there in the morning and she would take them home after she was finished with her work. The children did not do well in the nursery and the women did not want to send them there voluntarily. Thus, a child's attendance at the [village] nursery became compulsory.

The school in the village had only a seven-year course and most children who completed the course were fifteen years old. The school functioned well in the fall and spring seasons but it was shut down during the severest winter months.

We had our own wall newspaper. [A wall newspaper or a placard newspaper is a hand-lettered or printed newspaper designed to be displayed and read in public places both indoors and outdoors. They were tacked to vertical surfaces such as walls, boards and fences.] Most of the articles in the wall newspapers were devoted to the achievements of the government's five-year plans. There never was any real news. There were no articles about events that occurred in the Soviet Union or in other countries.

The only time we were told about foreign countries was on the May 1 celebrations. Then we listened to speeches that described the hunger that was suffered by people who lived in lands beyond our borders. We were told that there was little personal freedom in other countries and we were reminded that life in the Soviet Union was wonderful.

I realized that much of what the Soviet government had told me and my fellow citizens was not true after I was brought into Germany during the war. I was astounded by the kinds of farms that I saw in Bavaria. I was surprised that the farmers owned so many pigs, even the poorest farmers, and that the pigs appeared to be so healthy. The farms were well organized and they were run efficiently. This kind of farming did not exist in the Soviet Union.

Life was quiet in the villages where I worked. Though I was working for Germans who I did not like, I enjoyed the work. I felt the pure joy of tilling the soil, tending to the livestock and making things grow. I am a peasant and in the Soviet Union I was not allowed to be a peasant. I dreamed of owning a little farm, of owning pigs and other livestock. I knew that I would never be permitted to have this in the Soviet Union. With that in mind, I decided not to return to the Soviet Union.[1]

The authors do not know if Nikolai succeeded in fulfilling his dream which was to own a small farm which included agricultural land, farm equipment and livestock. We do not know if he succeeded in avoiding repatriation to the Soviet Union after the war. If Nikolai was repatriated, he would have been sent to a filtration camp where he would have been interrogated. If it was decided that he was guilty of collaborating with the enemy, he probably received either a death sentence or a sentence of ten years in prison. He was a traitor, guilty of treason, and was an enemy of the workers, an "enemy of the people."

It should be noted that at the war's end (The Great Patriotic War), more than 5 million Soviet citizens were living outside of the borders of the Soviet Union. At the Yalta Conference held in February 1945 in Yalta in the Crimea, the Allies: Prime Minister Winston Churchill of Great Britain, Franklin Roosevelt, President of the United States and Joseph Stalin representing the Soviet Union, agreed to help each other bring home the people who were their citizens but were living abroad. Soviet prisoners of war, Soviet citizens who had defected and Soviet civilians who had been brought to Hitler's Germany as forced laborers during the war, altogether some 3 million people, lived in areas in Germany controlled by British and American military forces. About 2 million lived in areas occupied by the Soviet military forces (the Red Army). Stalin demanded that all Soviet citizens who were living abroad, be returned to the Soviet Union.

By March 1946, over 4 million Soviet citizens had been returned to the Soviet Union. They had been repatriated. Upon their return, they spent several weeks in camps run by SMERSH agents and by agents of the NKVD. (see Glossary—SMERSH and NKVD) At these camps they were interrogated extensively. Thousands of returnees were sentenced to prison labor camps located in Siberia and more than a million were drafted into the Red Army or for labor purposes. More than 2 million were permitted to return to their homes.

During repatriation, a large number of Soviet citizens, labeled as displaced people, took measures to avoid being sent back to the Soviet Union. They did not want to return to Stalin's Soviet Union and Stalinism. Many claimed that they were Poles or citizens of a Baltic state. Because Poland was not part of the Soviet Union before the war, the British and American authorities did not recognize the Poles as Soviet citizens. Thus, the British and American authorities permitted them to stay in Western Europe. There were also displaced persons who, rather than returning to Stalin's Soviet Union, committed suicide.

Resistance to repatriation, persuaded the British and American authorities to reconsider the repatriation policy. General Dwight Eisenhower who initially supported the forcible repatriation policy gradually became appalled by the suicides among individuals who preferred to die rather than return to their native land. On September 4, 1945, he overstepped his authority and suspended the use of force in repatriation in the American occupation zone of operation. Two months later, British Field Marshal George Montgomery introduced a similar suspension in the British occupation zone. At the same time, Stalin continued to push for total repatriation and would do so well into the early 1950s.

## NOTE

1. Louis Fischer, *Thirteen Who Fled* (New York: Harper and Brothers, 1949), 191–197.

## Chapter 3

# Valentina Kamyshina

## *Married to an Enemy of the People*

"Enemy of the people" was a label that was applied to any opponent, real or imagined, of the Stalinist regime. It was simply anyone who was so designated by the Soviet authorities. Most of these people were sentenced under Article 58 of the Soviet penal (criminal) code. The code covered charges such as counter-revolutionary activity, armed uprising against the State, espionage activities against the State, acts of terrorism against Soviet organizations, and treason. Sentences for these crimes ranged from ten to twenty-five years of forced labor or execution. (see Document One)

Early on, a percentage of citizens who were labeled "enemies of the people" were given this label not because of their actions against the State but because of their social origin or their profession prior to the Bolshevik Revolution. That would include people who had hired labor or who had been high ranking clergy, or former policemen or merchants. During the famine of 1931 and 1932 peasants who spoke out against collectivization or who had tried to resist grain expropriations by the State, were labeled "enemies of the people." Peasants who were caught hoarding or hiding food so that their families would not starve, were labeled "enemies of the people." The withholding or theft of grain was declared, in the summer of 1932, a crime against the Soviet Union and therefore an act of political sabotage.

During the Great Terror of 1936–1938, many officials within the Russian Communist Party of the Soviet Union were charged with being "enemies of the people." Popular and loyal Old Bolshevik leaders such as Lev Kamenev, Grigori Zinoviev and Nikolai Bukharin were charged with being spies for capitalist nations. At their show trials, they admitted to being guilty of the fabricated charges that had been brought against them concerning anti-Soviet activities. They were executed. Millions of other Soviet citizens were also arrested under Article 58 of the Soviet criminal (penal) code and were executed or sentenced to do hard labor in a prison camp.(see- Document One)

31

The label "enemy of the people" carried with it a stigma for the families of the victims who were labeled as such. Wives and husbands of "enemies of the people" were removed from their places of employment and from their residences. They were expelled from the Russian Communist Party and from organizations identified with the Party such as the Komsomol. Children of "enemies of the people" were denied entry into universities and other institutions of higher learning. Generally, they could only find jobs at the worst kinds of employment. (see Glossary—Komsomol)

Valentina Kamyshina was the wife of an "enemy of the people." In March 1938, her husband was arrested and sentenced to ten years of imprisonment. She was not told the charge or charges that had been brought against him. When management at her place of employment learned that her husband was declared an "enemy of the people," she was fired and soon, thereafter, was evicted from her place of residence and forced to leave the city where she lived.

The remainder of the chapter contains Valentina's comments on the events in her life before her marriage and on the events that followed the arrest and imprisonment of her husband. The comments were made while she was being interviewed.


## VALENTINA KAMYSHINA'S COMMENTS

The story of my life is not unusual. Many Soviet women have had similar experiences.

When I was four years old, World War One began. During war, in 1917, the October Revolution [the Bolshevik Revolution], which brought the Bolsheviks to power in Russia, and the subsequent developments made little impression on me. [The October Revolution occurred on November 7, 1917, by the new calendar, the Gregorian Calendar, but on October 23 by the old calendar. That is why the Bolshevik Revolution was referred to by the Bolsheviks as the October Revolution. Vladimir Lenin and his Bolsheviks adopted the Gregorian Calendar after they came to power.]

As far as I know, the Bolshevik Revolution brought no significant hardship to my family. My parents had hoped to build a summer cabin; it was a dream they had for a long time. It would never become a reality but it was no great loss.

My family was small. It consisted of my father, mother, grandmother, sister and myself. Father was a railroad employee and held no important positions within the tsarist government. He belonged to no political party. Because of his heart disease, he had been exempted from military service. As a result, neither World War One nor the Bolshevik Revolution greatly affected my family. Of course, many people in Russia were killed during the war and during the revolution but that made little impression on me; I was only a child. Sometimes, during my evening prayers, my mother would tell me to pray for someone because he or she had died recently. But the deaths of these people caused me no sorrow. Materially, my family began to live less well, but even during the famine of 1920–1921, mother made sure that we did not go hungry.

It was through literature and the stories told by eyewitnesses that I became acquainted with the events that occurred during my childhood. I accepted the Bolshevik Revolution and with it the Bolshevik regime as developments in history. My parents often tried to prove to me that life in Russia was considerably better under the tsarist government; I argued endlessly that the opposite was true.

When I was eighteen, I married a talented engineer. Still quite young, he had already earned the degree of master of technical sciences and was preparing a thesis to earn a doctorate of technical sciences. He was a leading instructor in an institute. He was serious and very honest and he liked to keep to himself. He was in love with science and dedicated his life to it. My husband taught at three institutions of higher learning and he spent many hours working at home. At home he wrote a textbook as well as many articles that were published in technical journals.

Looking back, I find it remarkable that my husband was able to do the work that he accomplished at home. Our apartment was one small room in an eight-room house. One family lived in each of the rooms. There was a single kitchen that all the families were supposed to use. I didn't use the kitchen; I preferred to prepare our food in our room. My husband did his work through the noise of my cooking and my conversations with visiting friends.

Politics did not interest my husband. He accepted the Bolshevik Revolution although some of the policies of the Bolsheviks were not clear to him. Nevertheless, he did his work and carried out his responsibilities conscientiously. During our ten years together, I never heard him tell a political joke and that was very unusual in our time.

My husband had friends but he also had enemies. Most of his enemies were unsuccessful students. These were not students who had difficulty learning; they were students who did not want to study. The latter category [of students] consisted almost exclusively of Party or government people who were sent to universities for special training. They were people who had no preparation for the kind of [academic] work demanded of them at the university level.

My husband lost his father when he was fourteen years old. From then on, while attending high school and universities, he had to support his family which included two small siblings. His youth was spent running between a classroom and work and he was usually hungry. Despite this, he completed with excellence the work he was assigned in high school and at the universities.

That is why he could not identify with students who did not want to study. He often commented on how well students lived under the Soviets. They received a stipend and [free] living quarters; therefore, they should be able to study well. Comparing this with his own school years, he believed that his attitude was justified. He did not respect the student-Party members who viewed the university as a factory whose sole function it was to issue diplomas. The fancy official titles of such students did not scare him. His scrupulous honesty would not allow him to compromise. It was obvious that my husband's actions would cause him much unpleasantness. It is possible that it cost him his life.

On March 1, 1938, my husband was arrested and by the decision of a "troika" was sentenced to ten years of imprisonment under strict isolation and without correspondence privileges. Under what statute he was accused, I was never able to learn, despite my many appeals to magistrates and government officials.

When I received the announcement that my husband had been sentenced and was going to be sent to the Far North, I began to watch the prison trains that were leaving the city every night.

The nights were cold and it was raining. Maybe it did not always rain, but whenever I think back to those nights, the rain is always there. The trolleys had stopped running. One had to walk far distances to the railway stations. Every night, prisoners were shipped out from freight stations [located] at different ends of the city.

Since it was impossible for one individual to go to all the stations every evening, several wives of husbands who had also been sentenced to prison and I got together. Every evening we would meet and decide who would go to what station and there call out the names of all the husbands. Officially, what we did was forbidden. We were cursed by the guards who used vile language. Police dogs were directed at us. We were chased with bayonets. Sometimes we were shot at. But we continued to go out every evening, like one who reports to work. You go out but within you there is a coldness, an emptiness. There is no feeling in the heart. What was most horrible and frightening was that I prayed passionately to God that I would not see my husband. I was afraid with every fiber of my body to see him among the sad, bent figures with their hands behind their backs. I loved him. I was proud of him and that is why I did not want to see him degraded. I was afraid that if I did see him, something horrible would happen. I suffered this frightful feeling every evening that I went to see the prisoners leave. But I never saw my husband. Thus, my husband was taken out of my life forever. Other wives did see their husbands and some of the women fainted and went into hysterics. The guards cursed them and with their bayonets forced the prisoners to move along faster into the railroad cars.

At the place where I worked, I hid the fact that my husband had been arrested. I was listed as a divorced woman. It seems that I was never so gay and witty as at that time. I never had so many admirers as then.

I had to keep silent. I would have been fired immediately had the news of my husband's imprisonment reached the head office. My mother was ill and the care of my sister's little daughter had become my responsibility. If it became known that my husband was a prisoner, I would lose my job and finding another job would have been virtually impossible.

Days and nights passed and then everything came to a stop.

When the people in the head office learned that my husband was an "enemy of the people," I was fired. Soon thereafter, I was sent out of the city. Initially, with great effort and with the help of friends I was able to obtain various unskilled jobs. I was a scrub woman in a theater and I worked as a laundress. Later, I took up embroidery. I earned very little money at these jobs but they kept me occupied.

Not being able to obtain a real job in the town to where I was sent, I returned secretly to my mother and lived with her without police registration. To live in Soviet cities without police registration was risky. If discovered, one might be sentenced to prison for two years. Fearing the after dark check-ups by the police, I tried to stay awake throughout the night. I believe that if I had been left alone with my thoughts and had not kept myself occupied, I would have gone mad with fright. Doing embroidery calmed me.

Except for the fact that my husband had been sentenced to prison, I was never able to learn anything about his fate. Early in my search, I went to various administrative and judicial offices with the hope of getting some details. I finally decided to approach the prosecutor of the Republic. In my naivety, I believed that he would give me the information that I was seeking.

I arose early one morning and with a feeling of great excitement made my way to the prosecutor's office. I arrived there at eight o'clock although work did not begin until an hour later. When the office opened, I was escorted into a corridor-like small room. It was very cold and completely bare. Next to this room was the official reception room and occasionally, when the connecting door was opened, I caught a glimpse of a light, warm room with wonderful soft furniture.

Hours went by and the prosecutor eventually left to go for lunch. I was afraid to remind anyone of my presence fearing that I would not be permitted to see him if I seemed overanxious. My legs were numb from standing so long and my head ached.

Finally, at around seven o'clock in the evening, I was called into the prosecutor's office. Three or four people were in the room talking and laughing.

Of course, I was not invited to sit down. I began by asking the prosecutor to review my husband's case and I asked him to give me permission to remain in the city.

From his response, I realized almost immediately that I would learn nothing about my husband's whereabouts or wellbeing. Half-heartedly, he asked me questions.

"How long have you been married?"

"Ten years."

"And having lived with him for ten years, you did not know about his traitorous activities against Soviet authorities?"

I was tired. Nervous tension gave way completely to fatigue. Almost not understanding, I answered:

"He did not engage in traitorous activities; he was always very busy," and for some reason I added, "he was always very secretive."

Hearing that, the prosecutor came to life and smiled.

"There, you see! He was a secretive character and therefore a spy!"

What he said did not sink in immediately. But then a feeling of bitterness overcame me. I did not want to plead anymore; I couldn't. Looking straight at him I said:

"And comrade prosecutor, if my husband had been a sociable character, would he then have been labeled a counterrevolutionary?"

The other people in the room broke out into laughter. The prosecutor became angry. He then rose from his chair.

"I did not know about the case against your husband; we did not handle it. But I can tell you this, if your husband was accused of espionage, then nothing can help him."

Then he added with irritation:

"Why are you trying so hard to find out what your husband's crime was? What does it matter? Maybe he did nothing wrong. The action taken against him may have been totally prophylactic."

The interview was over and I walked out of the room. Out on the street, snow was falling softly. The evening was beautiful.

"Oh, my God! Oh, my God! Ten years under strict isolation. It was a prophylactic measure! Maybe he had done nothing . . . but his life is smashed. Why is it smashed? Maybe he had done nothing. PROPHYLAXIS, my whole attention centered on this word."

I saw this terrible word everywhere. With bloody letters it burned in the sky, over the street and on houses. I saw the word in the falling snowflakes. In every evening sound of the city, I heard the word. Prophylaxis, prophylaxis, it was in the hum of automobiles. Prophylaxis, I heard it in the trolley bells. It seemed to me that all the people on the street were repeating the word.

My mother came to meet me at the door.

"Mother do you know what prophylaxis means?"

She did not answer and asked no questions.

"Come on dear, come inside," she said gently taking my hand.

That night I broke out in a nervous, burning fever.

Gradually, I lost the desire to find out anything about my husband. All my attempts, my visits to Moscow and my constant trips to the NKVD had come to nothing. I came to realize that there was nothing that I could do. Now my only desire was to obtain permission to live in my native city with my mother. She was seriously ill and needed my constant attention and support.

At the prosecutor's office and at the NKVD office, I was often told the following:

"Why don't you get married? You are still young and beautiful. You should build for yourself a new life. But if you want to wait for your husband and hold on to his name then you might as well wait for him in the community where you were sent. We are sick of the mobs of women that crowd our reception rooms. If you should get married, then that will be a different matter. We will not break up a family. You will be allowed to live wherever you wish."

I was given this advice by my friends as well. Even my mother, who deeply loved my husband, told me:

"Marry again. It will be easier for you and your husband. Misha will not resent it. He is a good man; he will understand."

At first, I did not listen to such advice. I was frightened by the idea of marrying again. Then my hard, wearisome life caused me to reconsider especially after my last meeting with a high NKVD official. He told me frankly:

"I have turned down everyone of your written requests to permit you to change your place of residence. Now that you are here in person I will tell you directly, face to face, that until you marry again you will not receive permission to live where you want. There is no good reason for you to wait for your husband. Even if you do wait which would be a long time, and I don't believe you will, he will return to you as an invalid. You are a young woman."

The thought of my husband returning as an invalid did not concern me. No. I just wanted him back. I wanted to assist him and be useful to him. But to be able to do that, I needed to survive and save my strength. It already had been two years since my husband's arrest and I was exhausted. I longed for just one thing, to spend my nights in peace. It sounds odd but that is the way it was. I did not consider seriously taking my mother to a different town to start a new life. I did not have the energy. There was just one thing left for me to do and that was to take the step everyone had advised.

With great difficulty, I forced myself to apply for a divorce. I felt like a traitor. I was too ashamed to look at my husband's photograph. It seemed that there was reproach in his eyes.

Finally, I received my divorce. Now, I had to get married. It was a difficult action to take.

On the day that we were married, my new husband and I applied to the NKVD for permission to live in my native city. An affidavit was attached to the application certifying that my husband was a resident of the city and that he had a job there.

Several months went by and then I received a [letter of] refusal. I was stunned. Why a refusal? I was no longer the wife of an "enemy of the people." With great difficulty, I managed to get an appointment with the high NKVD official on whom my fate depended and who had advised me to get married. He smiled, looked at me condescendingly and said:

"You are strange! My advice to you was just a simple joke. You don't seem to recognize a joke."

For the first time in all of my visits to the many different offices, I burst out crying. What a joke! It was a terrible long-lasting joke.

I was dazed as I left the NKVD building. I walked a block or maybe two and then I sat down on a doorstep. I sat there for a long time, for several hours. My hopes were smashed and I recollected all the tortures that I had endured.

It was all just a joke.

Several months passed by and the war began, [the Great Patriotic War]. My situation became even more difficult. The spy mania in the Soviet Union and the desertions of the Soviet soldiers produced frequent searches. I spent days in the corner of the room not daring to go near the window and I would spend the nights in a secret cellar. My [new] husband had been sent to one of the military fronts. He had left as soon as the war began.

In time the German military forces arrived and occupied the city to which I had been assigned. I did not welcome their arrival; however, I breathed more freely. My secret existence ended with their presence.

A year later, I heard that my husband had been taken prisoner and a year and a half thereafter, I met him again in Germany. When the Germans withdrew from the city to which I had been assigned, I went with them [to Germany].[1]

The authors believe that the German occupation forces withdrew from the city as the Red Army forces were driving the Germans out of the Soviet Union and back to Germany. It is likely that Valentina, following Germany's surrender, was living in an area that would become part of the British occupation zone or the American occupation zone in Germany. It was in one of these occupation zones where Valentina was interviewed by a person or by people who worked for Louis Fischer, the editor of Thirteen Who Fled published in 1949.

# NOTE

1. Louis Fischer, *Thirteen Who Fled* (New York: Harper and Brothers, 1949), 102–110.

## Chapter 4

# Olga Minkevich

## *Raped by Stalin*

Stalin loved motion pictures and became deeply involved in the film industry in the Soviet Union. Often, after a late meeting with his inner circle of advisors, Stalin would ask them to join him at the Great Kremlin Palace cinema to watch a movie. The motion picture was selected by Ivan Bolshakov, Stalin's minister of cinema. If Stalin was feeling upbeat and happy, Bolshakov would show a newly produced Soviet film. If Stalin was feeling down or if he was irritated, Bolshakov would show an old classic or a foreign film.

Stalin had preferences and they varied. He loved motion pictures about American gangsters such as *Each Dawn I Die* starring James Cagney and George Raft. Stalin was also a big fan of Frank Capra's *It Happened One Night* starring Clark Gable and Claudette Colbert. He loved the Charlie Chaplin movies except for *The Great Dictator* and he enjoyed the Tarzan series starring Johnny Weissmuller.

Stalin's interest in movies was not limited to his regular viewings of films. Ever since the early 1930s, Stalin supervised every aspect of the Soviet Union's film industry. He was the ultimate censor, ordering films to be edited, remade or destroyed. He would suggest subjects, directors, actors and actresses and composers. He would read the scripts of proposed Soviet movies; he watched the rough cuts of those being made and he would order the insertion or the deletion of scenes and dialogues. When viewing *Volga-Volga*, a musical comedy, he was so shocked by a passionate French kiss scene that he had it cut from the film. For a while, thereafter, all kissing scenes were banned from all Soviet movies.

Stalin recognized the importance of motion pictures. Vladimir Lenin once said, "The cinema for us is the most important of the [fine] arts." It was a creed that Stalin believed. He realized that movies can be used to shape the way people think and he wanted the Soviet citizens to think of him as an all-knowing, benevolent leader. That is why Stalin interviewed every actor who portrayed him on screen. That is why he wholeheartedly approved of films such as *The Vow*. In it, Stalin is depicted receiving a blessing from Lenin's ghost as a sunbeam anoints his forehead. It is also why he hated movies such as Sergei Eisenstein's *Ivan the Terrible: Part 2*. In it the Russian tsar is portrayed as a mad, paranoid murderer. Stalin did not want the Soviet citizens to identify him with political rulers who had been ruthless killers.

One of the most important motion picture studios in the Soviet Union in the 1930s was Len Film studios located in Leningrad. It was at this studio that Olga Minkevich was paid to perform small acting roles in several films. Olga felt very fortunate to be given this opportunity because she desired to become a professional actress. It is highly probable that Stalin saw her in one of the many Soviet movies that he reviewed. It is very likely that he felt attracted to her and ordered her brought to Moscow and to his bedroom where he raped her.

In the paragraphs that follow, Olga recounted to the authors some of the more important events in her life. She survived the rape of Stalin. She survived her assignment to Leningrad's penal infantry battalion during the Great Patriotic War. She also survived her responsibilities as a Soviet military sniper stationed during the war near the Gulf of Finland killing Finnish snipers. For her actions as a sniper, Olga was awarded the "Order of Glory." The interviews with Olga were conducted in March 2010.


## OLGA MINKEVICH REMEMBERS

I was born on a freight train in 1922 while my parents were traveling to my father's new appointment in the Ukraine. [Olga's father was a military lawyer.] My birth was registered along the way at a railway station in the city of Dnepropetrovsk. We lived for quite some time in Rostov on the Don River and in 1930 we returned to Leningrad to the apartment where our ancestors had lived. The apartment was located on Vasiliyevsky Island. The apartment was so large that the State had it turned into a residence for six large families.

I received most of my formal education in Leningrad. I attended a school located on the 4th Line and studied acting at the House for Artistic Education for Children located on the 5th Line. I loved poetry and would memorize and recite my favorite poems. I still remember many of the longer poems.

I desired to be an actress and perform in films. One day, not far from Len Film studio, I was asked if I wanted to be in a film. "Sure I do," I replied. After that I was used in crowd scenes and given small roles in many movies. Even now, my friends will recognize me in a movie dating back to the 1930s. They will see me as a teenage girl in a crowd or acting out a minor role. I felt very fortunate to be given this opportunity and at the same time I was earning some money.

Mother did not like me working at Len Film studio because the work was usually done at night. Making a movie takes a lot of electricity and at that time in Leningrad there were electricity shortages during the daylight hours when many people were using electricity. Usually, my father walked me to Len Film studio and waited at the studio while I worked. But one night, I did not return from the studio. Nobody was able to explain to my father where I was or what had happened to me. [The authors believe that Olga was drugged by men who were given orders to bring Olga to Moscow and deliver her to Stalin's place of residence. The men were probably NKVD agents.]

When I recovered my consciousness, I was in the apartment of the leader of the world's proletariat, Comrade Joseph Stalin. I was in his bed and he was asleep in bed next to me. When I saw him, I became frantic. I knew about this apartment on Gorky Street, number 8 located in front of the famous restaurant "Aragvi." Soviet citizens knew that the members of the Soviet government would often meet and eat there.

I was desperate to leave immediately. But how could I do that? In the room there was a female guard who had been assigned to watch me. I saw her glance at my ears and I remembered that I was wearing antique diamond earrings, which were a gift from my grandmother. I realized that the earrings were my only means of escape. I offered the female guard the earrings if she would help me escape. She agreed.

It was towards the summer of 1941 just before the outbreak of the Great Patriotic War. I do not remember how I got to the railway station in Moscow. I was wearing a light summer dress and I had no money at all. I was told that a freight train at the station was going to depart and its destination was Leningrad. The train was loaded with firewood. Secretly, I climbed onto one of the freight wagons, hid myself among the logs and waited for the train to depart. From time to time, after its departure, the freight train would stop and I could hear someone banging on the wheels of the wagon with an instrument. During those times, I would not move fearing that I would be noticed.

After I returned to Leningrad, father explained to me what had happened after my disappearance. While he was waiting for me in the lobby of Len Film studio, a cleaning woman approached and said, "Oh! Maybe I will be shot for this, but I must tell you that some guys who I have never seen before treated your daughter with cakes and lemonade. I am sure that they have taken her to Moscow." The following morning father sent a telegram to the Kremlin in Moscow. The telegram read: "Give me back my daughter." I don't know if the telegram ever arrived in the Kremlin. However, soon thereafter father was summoned to the "Big House" [Bolshoy Dom] on Liteiny

Prospect. There, he was told that his daughter was okay and he should drop all attempts to get her back.

Days after I returned home, mother received telephone calls from people she did not know. They demanded that mother return her daughter to Moscow. Mother and father decided that the best way to protect me from Stalin was for me to get married. A marriage, in name only, was arranged between me and the son of my parents' friends. My birth name is Olga Kurnosova but on the marriage certificate I was listed as Olga Malis.

Just before the marriage was arranged, it was determined that I was pregnant. Since I had never had sexual intercourse before my encounter with Stalin, we concluded that Stalin had raped me and I was pregnant with his child. At that time in the Soviet Union, abortions were illegal. (See Glossary—Abortions in the Soviet Union) Nevertheless, my parents were able to locate a doctor who performed an abortion on me.

On June 22, 1941, we were informed that Germany had invaded the Soviet Union and we were now at war. I heard the announcement which was broadcast on a loudspeaker at one of the street corners. We had a family tradition of spending Sundays on the islands. [There was a huge recreation park at the northwest edge of Leningrad, on the islands of the delta of the Neva River.] Mother told me that Sunday morning [June 22, 1941], that I should go to the bakery on the 2nd Line and purchase a large apple pie and a big bottle of Kvass. I left and on my way to the bakery I heard the announcement. I was the first in the family to learn about the declaration of war. I was nineteen years old.

I do not remember much about the first months of the war. I do, however, remember the blockade [that was established against Leningrad by the Germans to the southwest and by the Finns to the north]. I remember the terrible hunger from which we suffered. Our family had no food reserves and we all suffered from scurvy. We all lost our teeth. We drank a lot of water to quiet the hunger pangs but as a consequence our bodies began to swell. Father was hospitalized and there he died.

Our primary source of food was our daily ration determined by the State and it was my duty each day to go to a State shop to get the family ration. On my walk home, I could not resist eating a little bit of the rather large piece of bread and I would tell my mother and sister, when I arrived home, that I had already eaten my portion.

We lived on Vasiliyevsky Island and the inhabitants of the island had one more source of food. It was a leather factory. The factory would receive from the Meat Processing Plant in the city the skins of the animals that were butchered. We would go to the factory and the State workers would give us some pieces of the skins. [These were probably pieces that could not be used to make items such as shoes.] After we cut away the wool, we boiled the skin for a long time until the water became a broth and the skin became a rubbery substance that we ate.

In time, I acquired a job as a nurse in a hospital on Vasiliyevsky Island. [At the time that Dr.Vinogradov interviewed Olga, she showed him the certificate that she was given which described her job responsibilities at the hospital and her job performance. She began her duties in July 1942 and proved to be a disciplined and hard worker. One of her duties was cleaning the city.]

To clean the city meant that we were to find the corpses of Leningraders who had died in the streets and to remove them. There were many corpses. It was not unusual to see a person walking ahead of you and suddenly fall down due to weakness and hunger. That person would be too weak to get up and would die where she or he had fallen. Others would walk by the fallen victim not daring to assist the victim fearing that they too would fall and be unable to pick themselves up.

Once, during the winter of 1941–1942, I walked to the Neva River to get water from a hole in the ice that had been made near the famous granite sphinx. [Due to the bombs dropped on the city by the Germans and due to the shelling of the city as well as the freezing temperatures, many of the water lines in the city were broken and the Leningraders were forced to get their water from the rivers that flowed through the city.] When I approached the ice hole, I saw a woman lying near the hole. The hem of her seal fur coat had been lifted and I saw that the meat from the upper parts of her legs had been cut off. Seeing that, I lost consciousness.

There was a little ship frozen in the ice not far from the ice hole. The military sailors on board that ship saw me fall and immediately left their ship to help me. They found my passport [an internal passport] which listed my place of residence on the 4th Line on Vasiliyevsky Island and they carried me home. If the sailors had not rescued me, I would have died at the ice hole.

Later, I was transferred to a military hospital to work as a nurse. At this hospital I was given soup, gruel and bread daily. I ate the soup and gruel and set aside the bread to give to my mother and sister. Then one day, the military commissar at the hospital asked me why I did not eat the bread. I explained to him that I was setting the bread aside to give to my mother and sister. "That's fine," he said. "When your work shift is over, you may go home to bring them the bread you have saved for them." (see Glossary—Commissar)

I was happy to see my mother and sister but my happiness was short-lived. Soon a Black Raven arrived at the family residence and I was arrested. [A Black Raven was a black vehicle that was used to transport a person under arrest to a local NKVD headquarters.] I was charged with being absent from my work without authorization. I was brought to the office of a military prosecutor located on Sadovaya Street. When I was questioned about my absence, I was unable to speak; I just cried. The three men who questioned me sentenced me to a prison labor camp for seven years. [Olga was viewed as an "enemy of the people."] They then changed the sentence and ordered that I become a Soviet soldier and join a battalion that was fighting along the military front. I was glad that they changed the sentence. I was not a Komsomol member, but I was a patriot and I desired to fight for my Motherland. Earlier, I had volunteered to join the military but because of my poor health I was deferred. (see Glossary—Komsomol)

From the military prosecutor's office, I was escorted to a military quarters. Though I was a prisoner-soldier, I was given permission to visit my family before being brought to the military front. The visit was to be brief, so I decided to catch a tram on Nevsky Prospect. [Nevsky Prospect was the main street in Leningrad.] I missed the first tram that I saw from a distance. I ran as fast as I could to catch it but the conductor did not wait for me. The tram left before I could reach it.

Fortunately, there arrived shortly thereafter another tram. I got on and after the tram had gone a distance down Nevsky Prospect, it suddenly stopped. The passengers were told that the tram could go no further. Apparently, the tram ahead of us, the one that I had tried to get on earlier, had been struck by a [German] artillery shell.

Soon after I returned to the military quarters, a large group of soldiers, including me, were sent to a military front. The front was not that far, so we were marched there. I distinctly remember the dirty roads and the monotonous sound of marching boots. The soldiers were not young [they were about forty years old or even older]. I remember that they sympathized with me and promised: "We will not permit you to perish at the hands of the enemy."

Our march ended when we reached the village of Nevskaya Dubrovka. There the Soviet forces had established a bridgehead called the Nevsliy Pyatachok [Nevsky Bridgehead] on the left bank of the Neva River. It was about two kilometers in length [along the Neva River] and 500–700 meters deep. The Soviet forces would defend the bridgehead from September 19, 1940 to April 29 in 1941 and would stop the Germans again from September 26, 1942 to February 17, 1943. I was told that the bridgehead was the most dangerous area within the Leningrad Front. From 40 thousand to 50 thousand Soviet soldiers lost their lives defending the bridgehead. My fellow soldiers were true to their promise to me. They did not permit me to perish at the hands of the enemy.

During my last fight at the bridgehead, I lost consciousness. When I finally regained my consciousness, I found myself lying in a bomb crater under the dead bodies of several of my fellow soldiers. They had perished during the fight and had fallen down on top of me. Only one of my legs remained uncovered and it was injured. I was returned to the military quarters in Leningrad.

In spite of my injury, I was sent to join a penal infantry battalion in Leningrad. [A penal battalion was a military formation consisting of soldiers who were declared guilty of an offense or offenses under a military law such as Order No. 227. Service in a penal battalion was considered a form of punishment. During a Soviet military offensive, the soldiers in a penal battalion were sent into battle first and directly into the minefields organized by the enemy. The penal infantry battalion would be followed in battle by the regular infantry units. If a member of a penal battalion should survive a series of battles, it was nothing but a miracle.] (see Glossary—Order No. 227)

The penal battalion to which I was assigned was stationed near the Pesochnaya railway station. [Olga joined the penal battalion on August 6, 1942.] It consisted of mostly military officers such as majors, lieutenant colonels and colonels. The battalion also included four women, me and three others. One of the women was sentenced to the penal battalion for having bartered some military bed linens for bread. She did this to prevent her children in Leningrad from dying of hunger. The other women had been sentenced to the penal battalion for similar crimes. [Each was an "enemy of the people."]

I survived, but only due to the orders of three men who arrived at our penal battalion. [The three men were probably interrogators representing the prosecutor's office in Leningrad.] They came to our battalion in an American car, a Villa, and asked the battalion commander if he had someone under his command with medical experience, someone who could provide an injured person with first aid. One of the three men had suffered an injury; a stray bullet had struck his hand. The commander knew that I was trained to be a nurse, so he called for me. When I arrived and began applying first aid to the injured hand, the other two members of the threesome began yelling at the battalion commander: "What are women doing here in a penal battalion? You must send them away immediately to a regular infantry unit."

The four of us were thus sent to a regular infantry unit. One was appointed to be a cook and another was assigned to wash and iron clothes. The company commander, because of my educational background, suggested that I learn to operate a mortar gun, an 82-millimter mortar gun. I agreed and I became the best gunner in our company.

After a while, I was trained to be a sniper and was transferred to a military unit stationed near the Gulf of Finland. There I was ordered to go hunting and most of my victims were enemy snipers. It was winter and the Finnish snipers would take aim at us from behind snow covered ridges [hummocks]. I was given a metal shield to hide behind.

It was on a sunny morning, when it happened. I shot a Finnish sniper; however, he shot his rifle at the same time that I fired mine. He probably saw the sun's reflection in the optical sight on my gun. His bullet hit the sight and

I suffered multiple wounds in my hand and my shoulder. For my actions as a sniper, I was awarded the Order of Glory.

After the war, I returned to Leningrad. I joined the Komsomol and worked as an instructor within the organization. I also got married. My husband graduated from the Electro Technical Institution and was assigned by the State to work in Moscow. Fortunately, I got a job in Moscow and this is where we lived until we returned to Leningrad twelve years later. This is where I would eventually retire.

In Moscow and in Leningrad Olga would share with others her encounter with Stalin which took place before the outbreak of the Great Patriotic War and her assignment to a penal infantry battalion during the war. But nobody believed her. "We," they would say, "never had something like a penal military battaion."

Their attitude changed after Nikita Khrushchev gave a speech in February 1956 to the Twentieth Party Congress of the Soviet Union. The lengthy speech initiated what became known as the de-Stalinization of the Soviet Union. Prior to de-Stalinization, most Soviet citizens had great respect for Stalin and admired the leader who had led them in victory over Hitler's Germany.

Finally, in 1984, Olga was recognized officially as a disabled war veteran.

*Chapter 5*

# The Great Patriotic War

As early as July 1940, Adolf Hitler decided that Germany should invade Soviet Russia in a military operation that he code-named Barbarossa. The objectives of the operation were defined in Directive No. 21, Operation Barbarossa, signed on December 18, 1940, by Hitler as the Commander-in-Chief of the Armed Forces. The directive stated that the "German armed forces must be prepared . . . to crush Soviet Russia in a rapid campaign." This was to be achieved by destroying the "bulk of the Russian army stationed in Western Russia" with "daring operations led by deeply penetrating armored spear-heads. Russian forces still capable of giving battle will be prevented from withdrawing into the depths of Russia." The final aim of the military operation was to form a defensive barrier against Asiatic Russia. The barrier was to extend from Archangel (Arkhangelsk) on the Arctic Ocean in the north to Astrakhan on the Caspian Sea in the south.

Operation Barbarossa was to be carried out by three German army groups, each supported by an air fleet. German Army Group North was to attack from East Prussia and take control of the Soviet Baltic republics and, with the military assistance from Finland to the north, destroy Leningrad. German Army Group Center was to be directed against Minsk, Smolensk and Moscow. German Army Group South was to attack on two separate wings, one from southern Poland and one from Rumania. They were to capture Kiev and invade and take control of the Donets industrial region and the Crimean Peninsula. In all, the German army groups were to total 145 divisions, of which nineteen were Panzer and fourteen were motorized.

It was decided that the German Panzer divisions in each army group would penetrate deep into the enemy's rear in wide encircling and enveloping movements so as to cut off all routes to withdrawal. The Panzer divisions would need assistance, initially, in breaking through the Red Army (the Soviet Army) defensive crust and for this reason an infantry corps was to be detached and put under the command of each Panzer division. The infantry corps was to make a rapid breach in the Red Army defenses, through which would then pour the Panzer division. The infantry corps would then revert to the command of its own army which would consist of primarily rifle divisions. It would be the responsibility of these divisions, as they made their steady advance, to destroy and mop up the encircled forces of the Red Army. (see Glossary—Red Army)

The conquered territories of Soviet Russia were to be occupied, administered and then exploited by Germany. As soon as the rear boundary of an army's zone of operations moved eastward in its military advance, the areas that had been overrun were to be occupied by German security forces. These forces were to prepare the native peoples for the political occupation that was to follow. The dual task of securing an area and preparing the native peoples for political occupation was assigned to Heinrich Himmler, the chief of all the police forces in Germany. He was to carry out the assignment independently of all other agencies and on his own responsibility. For the assignment, Himmler would create special task groups called Einsatzgruppen. The personnel of the Einsatzgruppen were chosen from the SS (Schutzstaffel), the elite guard of the National Socialist German Workers' Party, from the SD (Sicherheitts Dienste), the security and intelligence service, and from the Gestapo (Geheime Staatspolizei), the secret state police. They were to clear the conquered areas of all Jews, Communists and other racially and politically undesirable elements. A Himmler representative was to be assigned to each army group with an Einsatzgruppe at his disposal. The army group was to supply the men in the Einsatzgruppe with living quarters, food, fuel and other necessities, but the military was not to have control over them. The Einsatzgruppe was to follow directly behind the German troops as they advanced into Soviet Russia.

There was to be nothing benevolent about Germany's occupation and its administration of the conquered territories. Martial law was to be established. Native peoples who attacked members of a German army were to be killed on the spot. In circumstances where individuals attacking the German armed forces could not be readily identified, collective punitive measures were to be carried out immediately upon the orders of an officer with the rank of battalion commander or higher. Suspects were not to be retained in custody for trial at a later date. If members of a German army committed offenses against the indigenous population, prosecution was not to be compulsory even when their acts constituted crimes under German military law. Such acts were to be prosecuted only when the maintenance of discipline required it. All Russian Communist Party functionaries and Red Army commissars, including those at the small unit level, were to be eliminated not later than at the prisoner of war camps. Russian guerrillas were to be killed at any time.

Germany's ultimate goal in Soviet Russia was economic exploitation. With Soviet Russia's "boundless riches," as Hitler put it, Germany would be "unassailable" and would control the necessary potential for waging "future wars against continents." Russia's vast food resources were to feed the soldiers and people of Germany and Russia's raw materials were to be made available to the Four-Year Plan for Germany's economy. Hermann Goering, as commissioner of Germany's Four-Year Plan, was given jurisdiction over the entire program and was empowered to issue all orders concerning it, even to the German military. German needs were to be satisfied without any consideration for the native population.

In June 1941 the German High Command of the Armed Forces issued a directive for conducting propaganda during Operation Barbarossa. The people of Soviet Russia were to be told that the Germans were entering their country to liberate them from tyranny. They were to be assured that Germany did not consider them the enemy. However, if the population should offer resistance of any kind, the German armed forces would break it. The people were to be warned constantly not to participate in the fighting. It was to be impressed upon them to remain calm and orderly and to continue to "work as usual." They were to be made to understand that looting and the destruction of machinery and industrial installations would lead to poverty and famine. It was to be announced that collective farms were not to be dismantled (broken up) and that land was not to be distributed immediately to the people. This was to be done later. Several large newspapers were to continue to be published under German censorship. Similar use was to be made of radio networks. With the use of these media, special emphasis was to be given to policies that would produce a calming influence on the populace and dissuade them from committing acts of sabotage.

On June 22, 1941, Hitler ordered three large German army groups to invade and cross the Soviet Union's western frontier. The northern army group was directed toward the city of Leningrad. It was joined in the attack by Finland's military forces who were assigned to regain the territory that the Finns had lost to the Soviet Union in the "Winter War." A second German army group was directed toward Moscow and a third German army group was assigned to capture Kiev. Hitler's expectations of a quick military victory were not unreasonable. The Soviet Union's "Winter War" against Finland in 1939–1940 had revealed serious weaknesses in the structure and functioning of the Soviet military forces. This was due in part to Stalin's recent purges within the Soviet high command.

By mid-August 1941, all three German army groups were deep inside Communist Russia. German Army Group North was in Leningrad province and close to the city of Leningrad. German Army Group Center was approaching Moscow and German Army Group South had penetrated 563 kilometers (350 miles) into the southern area of the Soviet Union and it was approaching the Dnieper River.

In early November 1941, the city of Leningrad was almost completely encircled by the Finnish forces to the north and by the Germans approaching the city from the south. Together they established a siege against the city. In the south the city of Rostov was captured by the Germans and German Army Group Center had come within 40 kilometers (25 miles) of Moscow.

By late November vast areas in the Soviet Union were under German military control. Hundreds of thousands of Red Army soldiers had been captured and Soviet military casualties were enormously high. Yet, the Germans were not quite victorious.

In early December 1941, the arrival of an early Russian winter with sub-zero temperatures plus the Soviet military counteroffensives stopped the German military offensives. By mid-December, Germany's military commanders were calling for Hitler's permission to retreat. Hitler refused to sanction any significant military withdrawals. He believed that a full-scale withdrawal would most likely turn into an uncontrollable rout. All military units were ordered to stand where they were and, if necessary, to die there.

By the end of December, the Red Army military thrusts in both the north and the south gave signs that the Soviets were aiming to encircle German Army Group Center. Aware of the military catastrophe that threatened, Hitler ordered a limited military withdrawal in mid-January 1942. The withdrawal straightened the German front line and guarded the German troops against flanking attacks by the Red Army forces. Warm clothing was sent from Germany to the front line to protect the soldiers from the freezing temperatures. German reserve troops were also sent and when they arrived, they were moved into Germany's front line that extended from the city of Leningrad in the north to the Rostov-on-Don in the south.

Throughout the winter of 1941–1942 the city of Leningrad was besieged by the Finnish forces who were stationed to the north of the city and by the Germans to the south of the city. The Germans struck the city with incessant aerial bombing and with artillery fire using long-range guns. The bombs and the artillery shells caused the pipes of Leningrad's water system to burst. Thus, the rivers that flowed through Leningrad and the city's canals became the people's sources of water. A shortage of fuel in the city reduced the power supply which adversely affected the heating and the lighting of places of residence and the cooking of meals. But what was most devastating was the shortage of food in the city. Food supplies were airlifted, initially, into Leningrad and delivered on barges across Lake Ladoga located east of the city but this was insufficient to feed all the people. During the last days of November and throughout most of December the daily ration of bread was 250 grams for workers in factories and 125 grams for office workers, dependents and children. People ate whatever they could find to stay alive. Meanwhile the freezing temperatures deepened the ice that covered Lake Ladoga and made it possible to create ice roads across the lake. Food and other supplies were brought from the unoccupied Russian mainland to the east shore of the lake, transported across the lake on ice roads and then brought into Leningrad. The road of life, as it was called, helped save the city. Yet, thousands of its people would die from starvation. (see Map 1)

## Chapter 6

# Potential Enemies of the People

During the Great Patriotic War, the Soviet citizens who were Finnish in nationality and living in areas in the Leningrad Province that were not occupied by the Germans were rounded up by Stalin's regime, deported out of the province and exiled to areas in the eastern parts of the Soviet Union. Stalin feared that nationality groups such as Leningrad's Finns were filled with potential spies and saboteurs awaiting orders from their ethnic homelands. Spies and saboteurs were "enemies of the people."

The deportation of Leningrad's Finns began officially when, on August 26, 1941, the Military Soviet of the Leningrad Front issued Resolution No. 196ss which ordered the removal of the Soviet Finns from the Leningrad Province.[1] On August 30, 1941, the NKVD issued prikaz DO1175 "on measures for conducting the operation to resettle the Germans and Finns from the area of Leningrad to the Kazakh SSR."[2] Between August 31 and September 7, 1941, the NKVD deported 89,000 Soviet Finns from Leningrad Province to Kazakhstan.[3] The Military Soviet of the Leningrad Front then issued a second decision on the deportation of the Leningrad Finns.[4] On March 9, 1942, this body issued Resolution No. 00713 on removing the remaining Soviet Finnish population of the Leningrad Province to the Yukat ASSR, the Krasnoyarsk Kray and the Irkutsk Province.[5] On March 23, 1942, Stalin's regime deported Leningrad's remaining ethnic Finns. These Soviet Finns along with the others who had been deported and exiled before them would spend the remaining war years deep into the interior of the Soviet Union.

The eviction of all ethnic Finns living in the Pargolovo District within Leningrad Province was described in a letter that was addressed to the Executive Committee of Leningrad's City Council. The letter indicates that the victims had to leave behind most of their possessions and that some of the items were to be given to hospitals and orphanages. The rest were to be brought to State owned and operated stores and sold. The letter was written by the Representative of the Executive Committee of the District Council Deputies of all who work and it was dated March 30, 1942. It reads as follows:

55

We issued a detailed plan for each settlement and each echelon [a freight train consisting of many cars]. We recruited 173 persons: active members of the Party, officers of the NKVD and officers of the militia.

We notified the population about the evacuation [their eviction from the Leningrad Province] 24 hours before they were to be evacuated [evicted]. Sometimes they were given only a 6- or 8-hour notice.

At a specific time, the evacuees were taken to the railway station. When a train was delayed, the evacuees had to wait for 10 or 12 hours. As a result, there were huge crowds of people at the railway station. But the loading of the trains was well organized.

During the length of the evacuation there were no accidents; no anti-Soviet or counter revolutionary comments were voiced by the evacuees. The possessions left by the evacuees were described. But the most valuable possessions were damaged by the evacuees. For example, bicycles were missing their chains and sewing machines were missing their thread spools.

Each cow that was owned by the evacuees was handed over to the State in exchange for a document promising the owner that the State will return to the person another cow. We took from the evacuees 599 cows, 2 goats and 23 horses. We also took from the evacuees 15 tons of hay and 250 kilograms of potatoes. The cattle and hay were distributed among the Soviet collective farms according to the decision made by the Leningrad Provincial Council. The potatoes were given to the organization which deals with the gathering and selling of fruits and vegetables to be distributed to the population.

The private possessions of the evacuees were placed in special storage. Each item was appraised and its value was determined in rubles. Some of the possessions were given to children's houses [orphanages] and to hospitals and the rest of the items were given to stores to be sold to consumers.

During the three-day evacuation [eviction], March 26, 27 and 28, it was determined that 13,875 people were evacuated. Approximately, 200 people were not evacuated because they were ill or could not be found.

Generally speaking, the evacuation in the district was well organized.

[Signed by]
Representative of the Executive Committee of the
District Council of Deputies of all who work

(signed) Velikodvors

## EILAH VANKHANEN: EXILED FINNISH RUSSIAN

Eilah Vankhanen and her granny and little brother lived in a village-collective farm which was located in the Pargolovo District. Because they were ethnic Finns, they were ordered to leave their homeland (the village-collective farm) and appear at the railway station (in Toksovo) within twenty-four hours. In the paragraphs that follow, Eilah describes the events that she experienced during her removal from Leningrad and during her exile to Siberia:

My childhood was difficult. My mother died in 1932 and father passed on in 1936. My brother and grandmother and I were brought to a collective farm and we became the farm's responsibility. I was just thirteen years old at that time.

In 1940 I became an assistant to the accountant of the collective farm. But shortly thereafter, the farm's accountant was transferred to the Machine Tractor Station within the district. It meant that I would have to do the accounting for the farm alone. I had only a six-year education and four of those years were in the Finnish language. Nevertheless, I managed to do my job and needed and received assistance only with the annual reports.

When the war broke out, the young people in our district, the Pargolovo District, were recruited to construct lines of defense, airfields and anti-tank trenches. [The Pargolovo District was a district located in the northern part of Leningrad Province.] On the first of July 1941, I, and other teenagers between the ages of 17 and 19 were sent north to construct a line of defense against Finland. Later, in August [1941], we were brought to Muartcmyagi to construct a runway for Soviet aircraft. It was hard work. I still remember the names of several of the young people within the group of workers: Toyvo Vasilyev [Finnish first name, Russian last name], Maria Aleksandrova [Russian first name, Russian last name], Miska Kourginen [Russian first name, Finnish last name], Misha Kanninen [Russian first name, Finnish last name], Anna Myagyalyainen [Russian first name, Finnish last name] and Elma Varayeinen [Finnish first name, Finnish last name].

The work became more difficult after we were brought to Toksovo. There we dug anti-tank trenches. The ground was heavy meaning that it contained lots of rocks and clay. It is difficult to spade clay especially in the winter when it is cold. Before we shoveled the dirt, we had to break it up with long steel rods. To do that kind of work, a person needs to be fed nourishing meals. We were given a thin barley soup.

From time-to-time, Soviet soldiers from a nearby garrison would steal some of our food reserves. [Military garrisons were stationed in various locations within the Soviet Union. These garrisons were ordered to look for and capture parachutists who had been dropped by the enemy in locations behind the Soviet military front line. The soldiers in these garrisons were not fed as well as the soldiers fighting along the front lines.]

In November [1941] we were brought to still another area to load peat onto railroad cars. The peat was brought into the city of Leningrad where the people were suffering from the blockade. Our group of workers was joined by teenagers from nearby villages. Three of them were sisters with the last name Radikainen [Finnish name] and two were sisters with the last name

Taude [Finnish name] and there were several boys. We worked twelve hours a day whether it was snowing or not. Sometimes, the workday was longer than twelve hours; it depended on the arrival of the trains. It was hard work especially during a snowstorm or when it was extremely cold. But we were fed rather well. We were given bread, gruel, soup and sugar and we became alive like flies in the spring.

Our village [the collective farm] was located approximately twenty-five kilometers [15 miles] from our work site. So, periodically we would walk home to be with relatives and friends. Sometimes, I would take home some bread and sugar to give to my brother and granny.

On March 27, 1942, I arrived in our village late at night and discovered that the village was virtually empty. Almost all the villagers had been moved out. There remained in the village only my brother and granny and the parents of Lisa Kyarginen [Finnish last name]. These people had been left because they were too weak to be evicted. [Eilah's village-collective farm was inhabited primarily by ethnic Finns.]

That same night, two men on horseback arrived in the village and they ordered us to leave as soon as possible. The train that we were to board was waiting for us at the railway station in Toksovo. The men on horseback told us that each person was permitted to take thirty kilograms [66 pounds] of items. It meant that we had to abandon almost all of our possessions including my mother's sewing machine. Later on, I would often think of that sewing machine because we had need of it. It was a shame to leave it as well as our other possessions. I placed granny on a sled and pulled her to the railway station. We arrived at the station that night and early in the morning of March 28, 1942, we were placed on a passenger train and transported to the western side of Lake Ladoga. There we climbed into the rear bed of a truck which brought us across the ice-covered lake and to the opposite side. On March 29, 1942, we were boarded onto a freight train which was to take us east into Siberia.

The trip to Siberia was marked with difficulties. We were provided good meals on the train but many people did not survive the trip. In our freight car there were 125 people but only 92 survived. My granny was one of the people who died and my little brother was lost. I do not know what happened to him. I was alone. In Omsk, three of the freight cars were cut loose and I was in one of them. The rest of the train moved on. Those of us who were left at Omsk were brought to different places and assigned work. When the ice covering the Ob River melted, we were brought by barge to a fishermen's village located about 80 kilometers [50 miles] from Salekhard which was a rather large community in Siberia.

I remained living in Siberia until 1949, when my husband and I and our two daughters moved to the Republic of Karelia. I was married in 1944 and gave birth to my oldest daughter in 1946 and my youngest daughter in

1949. At first, we lived in a state farm named Salmi where I worked as an accountant like I had back when I was a teenager. Then in 1958 we moved to a village named Meliorativny where my husband worked as an operator of an excavator. Now I am retired and I am provided with a pension and all the privileges awarded to the citizens of Leningrad who survived the blockade against the city.

## M. MAHLINEN: ETHNIC FINN
## EXILED UNDER STALINISM

Like Eilah Vankhanen, M. Mahlinen was an ethnic Finn who was deported from Leningrad Province and transported to Siberia. On March 22, 1942, she and her family, living in a collective farm, were told that early the next morning they were to be evicted from their residence and transported to the city of Leningrad. From there they were to be brought to the western shore of Lake Ladoga and then by truck across the ice-covered lake to the eastern shore. When they arrived at the eastern shore of the lake, they were to be loaded on a freight train which would bring them into Siberia. In 2013, Malinen described in detail the events that took place during the trip. She also recounted the difficulties that she and her family suffered due to Stalin's policies. These are recorded in the following paragraphs:

Limuzi was the name of our village and it was located along the southern shore of the Finnish Gulf within Leningrad Province. Our house was beautiful and well-constructed. It was surrounded by trees which included birches and poplars. We also had cherry and apple trees and raspberry, currant and gooseberry bushes. The trees and the bushes were especially beautiful in the spring when they were colored with flowers. My parents lived there for many years; they loved nature and were happy with their farm. From the windows of their house, they could see the waters of the Finnish Gulf and the island of Kronshtadt. My parents had built much of what they owned and in the 1920s our family was classified as being "middle class."

In 1930 our family joined a newly organized collective farm. My parents had no choice in the matter. The State authorities claimed that those "who are not with us—are against us." [They would be "enemies of the people."] The State took our horse, our cow and all of our seeds and these became the ownership of the collective farm. As a consequence, our family became poor.

When the war came to the Soviet Union in 1941, our family would suffer disgrace through the decisions made by Stalin's regime. In March 1942, Stalin's government [the State] decided that the ethnic Finns were to be evicted from their homelands. The ethnic Finns living in Leningrad Province were to be moved to the northeastern area of the Soviet Union. On 22 March, it was announced that we must be ready to leave our residence early the next morning. Each person was permitted to take luggage but it must not weigh more than 30 kilograms [66 pounds]. We had received no advanced warning about our eviction and we were not prepared for the long transport to a location in the northeast. In the morning, several military trucks arrived and all the ethnic Finnish families in the collective [farm] were loaded on the trucks. Our family consisted of my parents who were already retired, my sister and me. I had two brothers but they had already been drafted into the military.

The military trucks transported us to the island of Kronshtadt using the road that had been organized across the ice that still covered the Gulf of Finland. From Kronshtadt we were delivered to the village of Lisiy Nos along the northeast shore of the gulf. From there we were brought to Leningrad and without any delay we were brought to the western shore of Lake Ladoga and transported across the lake using the famous "Road of Life," a road organized across the ice that covered the lake. On the eastern shore of the lake, a train was waiting to transport us to Siberia.

It was a freight train and we were driven like cattle into a freight car. The car was furnished with an iron stove which burned wood and bunk beds made with wood planking that were placed against the walls. There were not enough beds to accommodate all the people in the car, so our family was told to sleep on the floor underneath the planking of the bottom beds. This is how we were brought to Siberia for the next month and a half. Within the freight car there were old women and men, and young women with babies and children. Everyone in the freight car had been evicted from their homes.

The conditions in our freight car were terrible. We were constantly hungry and we were not given enough water. Whenever the train stopped at a railway station, we were urged to go under the freight car and look for water. There were some who were still under the train when the train began moving; these people perished under the wheels of the train. In our freight car a 16-year-old girl lost her leg beneath our car. People became ill with dysentery because of the dirty water.

Due to the overcrowded and unclean conditions, people became ill with typhus. If they died, their bodies were removed from the freight car when the train stopped at a large railway station. When we arrived at the railway station in Krasnoyarsk, it was announced over the loudspeaker that a trainload of people suffering from typhus had just arrived. The people at the station were being warned about us. No one in our family had typhus and I am convinced that God protected us.

We were told to get off the train in Kitai within Irkutsk Province. We were brought to a lumber mill and there we worked for three months. We were then brought to the city of Yakutsk where we were disinfected. After our disinfection, we were transported back into Irkutsk Province to harvest potatoes and cabbages. Eventually, our family was assigned to a collective farm that had been organized around a village named Sinsk. The weather turned severely cold and during the winter father died.

In March 1943, I addressed a letter to the local Communist Party Committee asking them to help me get a job. I informed them that I had graduated from the Leningrad Institute of Soviet Trade Management. Their reply was astonishing; they offered me the position of manager over the food storage of a town named Pokrovsky. I took the position and after working in Pokrovsky for three years, I was given permission to move to Yakutsk.

In Yakutsk I began working as an economist within the administration which was in charge of the city's canteens. I worked at that position success-fully for two weeks until I was fired. I was fired because I was an ethnic Finn and the authorities of the Republic did not trust ethnic Finns.

My next job post was within the administration of the textile industry. After two weeks, my boss was summoned by the Ministry of Trade and was reprimanded for hiring me. "How could you hire this 'White Finn'? She is not to be trusted." My boss was an upright person and told them that I could not be a "White Finn" because I was born in the Soviet Union and I had studied in Soviet institutions of learning. My boss refused to fire me and I have been deeply grateful to him ever since. I worked in the textile industry from 1948 until 1991. During that time, I earned several awards and was awarded the title "Veteran of Trade."

My sister Katherine lives with me. For the past twenty-five years she worked at the Republic Sanitary-Epidemiology Station. Her life has been long and hard but not as hard as my two brothers.

My older brother, Peter, went into the military. After graduating from a series of officer courses, he became a lieutenant in the Red Army. But after the war broke out, he was dismissed and sent to Siberia where he was forced to work at a military factory. There he lost his left arm as a result of an accident. Following the war, Peter tried to return to our "Motherland" the village of Limuzi along the southern coast of the Gulf of Finland but because he was an ethnic Finn the authorities would not grant him permission. Peter went to Kazakhstan instead and worked as an engineer. There he died in 1980.

My younger brother was also dismissed from the Red Army and was sent to the Komi Republic and then to the Chelyabinsk Province in Siberia. There he worked in a coal mine and lived in extreme poverty. He had little to eat and sometimes he was so weak physically that he could not go to work. It was a friend who rescued him from this horrendous situation. My brother then worked as a turner at a machine repair factory.

Mother hoped to see her sons before she died but that did not happen. She died in Yakutia in 1955.

In 1993 the ethnic Finns in Russia were "rehabilitated" and were permitted by law to return to their "Motherlands." (see Glossary—Soviet Rehabilitation) No one in our family returned to Limuzi, our "Motherland," because it would mean that we would have to buy land and build a house. We had lost our land during collectivization and we lost our house during the war [The Great Patriotic War]. Thus, I remained living in Yakutia.

## NOTES

1. J. Otto Pohl, *Ethnic Cleansing in the USSR, 1937–1949* (Westport, Connecticut: Greenwood Press, 1999), 24.

2. Pohl, *Ethnic Cleansing in the USSR, 1937–1949*, 24.

3. Pohl, *Ethnic Cleansing in the USSR, 1937–1949*, 24.

4. Pohl, *Ethnic Cleansing in the USSR, 1937–1949*, 24.

5. Pohl, *Ethnic Cleansing in the USSR, 1937–1949*, 24.

## Chapter 7

# Ganadi Danilov

## *Transported to Finland*

The people of Pakhomovka did not immediately learn about the invasion of the Soviet Union. Pakhomovka was a village located on the Soikino Peninsula in the province of Leningrad. Almost all the villagers were ethnic Finns who spoke both Russian and Izhovian; however, their first language was Izhovian (a Finnish dialect). Historically, the men in the village were fishermen catching their fish in the southern waters of the Gulf of Finland. In 1935 the village was turned into a collective farm and from that time forward until the outbreak of the war (Great Patriotic War) the villagers were expected to grow and raise agricultural products as well as catch fish. Ganadi Danilov and his father, Nicholas, were two native villagers who fished the waters of the Gulf of Finland.

In the summer of 2011, the authors met with Ganadi Danilov and he shared with them his recollections. Ganadi was thirteen years old when the Germans arrived in Pakhomovka in 1941. He remembered what life was like in the village before the war and what it became like under German occupation during the war. The following account is a compilation of Ganadi's recollections:

My father, Nicholas Danilov, was a very good fisherman. Father considered himself skilled and in 1934 purchased special fishing equipment. The traditional fishing nets consisted of just fifty squares but the newer nets were larger having from seventy-five to one hundred squares. With the newer nets a person was able to catch more fish. Father also owned a mobile fishing hut which he used on the ice that covered the Gulf of Finland during the winter season. The fishing hut was a rectangular wooden building that was built on two rails. Inside the hut there was a small stove. A rather wide plank bed was constructed to each wall so that four people could sleep in the hut. The hut was pulled out onto the ice by our horse. When father arrived at the spot where he wanted to fish, he protected the animal from the cold wind that blew across the gulf. He organized a temporary shelter made of hay. Father then made a large hole in the ice and dropped a net through the hole and into the icy water. After a while, he would retrieve the net. The fish that were caught in the net were thrown onto the ice. Father would spend the entire day fishing.

In 1935 our village, Pakhomovka, was turned into a collective farm. I was seven years old when this was done. All the people in the village were ordered to become members of the newly established farm. The person who joined the collective farm would have to give to the farm most of his private possessions. Father did not want to give up his fishing equipment and refused, initially, to join the collective farm. The newly appointed chairman of the farm was a committed Communist. He, like my father, was an ethnic Finn. He did not know how to read or write the Russian language and could not converse using the Russian language. He approached my father and in Izhovian he urged father to become a member of the collective farm. "Nicholas," he said, "I warn you that if you do not enter the collective farm, you will lose everything." There were many in our village and in neighboring villages who refused to join a collective farm. These people were rounded up and sent under armed guard to Kazakstan. Father responded to the chairman's warning by pacing forth and back in the living room of our house. He finally made the decision to join the collective and on the following morning reported officially that he would become a member. Immediately, thereafter, all of father's fishing equipment was confiscated and it became the property of the collective farm.

The farm was given the name of our village, Pakhomovka. It was named after P. Pakhomovka, a revolutionary who participated in the Bolshevik Revolution also called the October Revolution. (see Glossary—October Revolution) Before the revolution our village was called Vodsky Konetz. [The translation is "This side of Vod." The name Vod refers to a Finnish tribe.]

The collective farm produced agricultural products, milk, beef and fish and much of this food was brought to the city of Leningrad. The members of the farm were required to participate in all the production activities. Thus, a family would be assigned to fish one week and in the following week be required to tend to the cows and other livestock owned by the farm.

The members of the farm became as poor as church mice. During the year before the war [1940] my parents worked all year long and received from the collective farm only sixteen kilograms of poor-quality rye. Together, my parents had earned credit for many workdays but they received in return very little. There was no private ownership of horses. All the horses on the collective farm belonged to the farm. Our family did own a cow but we were required to pay the State a tax on the cow. The tax was paid by giving the State a portion of the milk produced by the cow and a portion of the butter that we made from the milk. If the tax was not paid, our cow would be confiscated. There were eight children in our family and we needed all the milk produced by our cow. The State also demanded that each family pay annually, as a tax, fifty eggs even if the family did not own chickens. The State also imposed a tax on families that owned fruit trees. We owned some apple trees but my granny cut them all down except one so that the family would not have to pay a large tax on the apple trees.

There was no policeman in the village. There lived in our village a naval commandant and he had an office in the village. He was responsible for maintaining civil order. There was also a security guard who walked the streets of the village at night. If a fire should start, he would alert the families who were in danger and others in the village who were able to fight the fire.

Religion was prohibited and the church in the village was destroyed. One day the chairman of the collective farm tied some long ropes to the cross that surmounted the village church. He then tried to pull down the cross with a tractor. The cross did not come down; it only bent forward. A little later, the chairman went into a sauna bathhouse to bathe. The flue in the smoke duct of the stove was closed and the chairman became asphyxiated. When he lost consciousness, he fell onto the hot stove. His naked body was burned severely and several days later the chairman died. [Ganadi believes to this day that the chairman suffered an early death as punishment from God for what he had done to the village church.]

Before religion was outlawed in the Soviet Union, our family worshipped as Russian Orthodox Christians. Every member of the family was baptized and the family owned two icons. (see Glossary—Icon) The icons were acquired by father during the Bolshevik [October] Revolution when he was a sailor in the Russian Baltic Fleet. When the revolution broke out, father and his fellow sailors mutinied, removed their officers and established control over their ship. They also removed all the icons from the ship. Each sailor was given permission to keep one or two of the icons but the rest were thrown away. Father took two of the icons, one bearing the image of St. Nicholas and the other of St. Mary. Father chose these two icons because his name was Nicholas and my mother's name was Maria. The icons were hung in one of the corners inside our house. [Ganadi has the two icons hanging in his house today.]

Hitler's forces arrived in Pakhomovka shortly after we were told that Germany had invaded the Soviet Union. A few Germans on motorcycles entered our village initially and they left as quickly as they had entered. [The village was the hub of the collective farm.] The Germans had come into the village to determine if there were Red Army soldiers in the village.

The only fighting that I witnessed during the war were a few air combats. One day a German airplane appeared in the sky and dropped its bombs. A Soviet aircraft went in pursuit of the German airplane but the Soviet aircraft was shot down. A second Soviet aircraft went in pursuit but it too was shot down. The next day the German airplane appeared again but on this day it was met by two Soviet fighters flying together. There was some air combat but it ended when the German airplane retreated to the sea. The German pilot dove down to just above the surface of the water as if his airplane had been hit and crashed into the sea. The Soviet fighters did not pursue the enemy airplane believing it had crashed. It, in fact, had not.

Our way of life changed under German rule and we enjoyed greater freedom. The collective farm was dismantled and the village families divided the agricultural land among themselves. The fish that father caught, we were permitted to keep. The Germans did not place a tax on the food that we produced or caught. They did require that we remove the snow off the main road. This was not difficult nor was it time-consuming because there were many people clearing the road and the surface of the road was rather smooth. I remember working on the road only three times and each time it was after a snowfall.

The Germans tried to enforce certain restrictions. For example, they established a boundary line on the ice covering the Gulf of Finland; it was about one kilometer from the shoreline. The boundary line was marked with poles anchored in the ice. The fishermen of our village and from the neighboring villages were forbidden to fish beyond the established boundary line. If a person went beyond the line, he might escape from the German occupied territory. There were islands just eighteen kilometers [11 miles] from the shoreline and these islands were still under Soviet control. The Germans did not want us to escape to these islands.

Father refused to fish in the area that had been marked by the Germans. There were hundreds of fishermen in the area and there were too many fishing nets. Father decided to go beyond the established boundary line. He took with him a fishing net which consisted of one hundred squares and it was fifty meters long [54 and a half yards long]. It was a net that had belonged to the collective farm but now it belonged to father. He had no fishing hut, so he took a large piece of canvass and used that to construct a makeshift shelter. I would go along with father and together we made our holes in the ice.

Once, while we were fishing beyond the established boundary line, the Germans on patrol saw us and began to approach us. We ran from them. They shot in the air and ordered us to stop but they did not try to shoot us. When they reached our nets, they tried to release them and get them to drop to the bottom of the sea. The nets did not sink and after the Germans left, father and I were able to retrieve them. If the Germans had caught us, they probably would have penalized us in some way.

I discovered that the Germans were different from each other. Some were as cruel as beasts but others behaved as kind human beings. I remember one German soldier who came to our house. When he saw that there were eight children in our family, he took from his pocket a photograph of his family.

He had a wife and two children. They were clean and were well dressed, not like us. I cannot recall an incident when the Germans, who were stationed in Roochiyi, entered our village demanding that we give them food. I do remember villagers walking from Pakhomovka to Roochiyi, a distance of two kilometers [1.2 miles], to barter fish, milk and eggs. The Germans in turn gave them items such as bread that was packaged so that it would remain fresh for a long time.

We were brought to Estonia when the Germans evacuated us from our village. They transported us in freight cars. We were not told where they were taking us. When our train stopped, we were in Tallin and we knew we were in Estonia. From Tallin we were brought to Paldiski which was a large Estonian port where the Germans had organized several concentration camps. As we entered the camp where we were to be held, we noticed mounds of corpses. The Germans had taken those who had died in the camp and stacked them in rows and placed between the rows of corpses, rows of small tree trunks. These mounds of human bodies were to be torched and burned. I was surprised that the Germans allowed us to witness the mounds.

The living conditions in the camp were not good. The food that they fed us was soup prepared in large kettles. It caused some to become ill and die. The first to die in the camp were the oldest and youngest inmates. In time my family was given a choice; we could choose to go to Finland or to be brought to Germany. We chose to go to Finland.

When we arrived in Finland, we were held initially in a concentration camp. Our sleeping quarters consisted of beds, stacked three levels high, which were made of wooden planks. The attitude of the camp guards was quite good. We were given the opportunity to wash ourselves in a bath house two to three times a week. At the same time, we washed our clothes in order to avoid getting lice. The food that was prepared for us was much better than what we received in Estonia.

The camp was visited by Finnish farmers who were in search of workers. We would not be hired for a long time. Our family was large. There was my mother and father and eight children. There was only one good worker in the family and that was father. I was the oldest child within the family and I was just fifteen years old.

A kind man finally hired the family and brought us to his farm. He shared his house with us. Half of the house was used by his family and the other half was occupied by us. He expected us to work hard but working hard was nothing new to us. Back in the Soviet Union we were forced to labor on the collective farm from sunrise to sunset. The farmer paid us by providing us with a place to sleep and by feeding us. Sunday was the day of rest and the farmer did not force us to attend worship services held in church.

On Sundays father and I would walk to the nearby port and hire ourselves out. Freight ships at the port needed to be loaded and unloaded. It was Sunday and we were paid extra, twice the amount that a worker on the docks earned on each of the other days of the week. If we worked a ninth hour on Sunday, our pay for that hour would be doubled. I remember being given documents such as passports. We were permitted to walk about freely. We were able to understand the native Finns quite well, although a number of the words that they used were unfamiliar to us.

Our stay at the farm ended after a person representing the Soviet Union arrived at the farm. The representative asked us if we wanted to stay in Finland or return to the Soviet Union. My family wanted to return home. Life was good in Finland. We ate better and we were dressed better in Finland than in the Soviet Union, yet Russia was our Motherland and we wanted to return to our Motherland.

On the day of our departure, the kind Finnish farmer tried to persuade us to stay in Finland. He asked us where we were going to live once we arrived in the Soviet Union. "You have neither a house nor property," he said. "Stay here; I will give you a house and a cow. Please stay." "No," we told him, "we want to go home." So, the kind man provided us with a large box which we filled with our possessions. He then helped bring us to the nearby railway station where we were scheduled to board the train that was to bring us home. At the station we saw many other Soviet citizens who were returning home. They were singing songs, playing music and smiling and laughing. They were happy to be going home.

When we arrived in Yborg a member of the NKVD entered our railroad car to tell us that we would not be going to the Soikino District. [The Soikino District was located within Leningrad Province and the village of Pakhomovka was located in the Soikino District.] He said that everything in the district had been destroyed. He said that we would be brought to Yaroslavl Province and we would stay there but only temporarily. We then departed for our new destination. Some would not arrive in Yaroslavl Province; they escaped with the intention of returning to Finland. These were young people, both male and female, who were in their early twenties.

Five days after we arrived in Yaroslavl Province, father was arrested by the NKVD. (see Glossary—NKVD) He was found guilty of being an "enemy of the people" and was sent to a prison camp. His sentence was ten years. The sentence was based on two charges. Father was the village elder of our village during the time when the Germans occupied our district. Father was accused of collaborating with the enemy. Thus, he was a traitor and an "enemy of the people."

Father was also accused of desertion. Father was drafted after the war began. He went into the military but shortly after he was inducted, he became ill. He was sent home. By the time he recovered from his illness, the district in which we lived had been overrun by the Germans and the Germans were occupying the area. There was a law in our country which pertained to all males who were old enough to be in the military. "If you are old enough to be a soldier [from 20 to 45 years old] then you must be in the Red Army." If you should come across an enemy, you must kill him. If you are unable to do so, then you must kill yourself. That is why Soviet soldiers who were captured by the enemy and who became prisoners of war were sent to Soviet prison camps upon their return to the Soviet Union following the Great Patriotic War. According to law, they should have committed suicide rather than allow the enemy to capture them.

Ganadi's father was sent to the prison camp in Kalima and he returned to his family after he served his ten-year sentence. This "enemy of the people" had been rehabilitated while in prison. (see Glossary—Soviet Rehabilitation) He did not return to Pakhomovka or to the Soikinskiy District. No ethnic Finn was permitted to return to the district until 1955. If an ethnic Finn did return, that person was given permission to stay for twenty-four hours and then he or she had to leave. Ganadi's father would eventually live in Kyovstovo and that is where he was buried.

When the authors met with Ganadi in 2011, he was living in a village near Kingisepp. The village is located in what used to be Leningrad Province. One could say that Ganadi had returned to his homeland. He talked about fishing and the methods that his father had used to catch fish on the ice of the Gulf of Finland. Ganadi and his family suffered much following their return to the Soviet Union from Finland, yet he did not seem bitter. He appeared strong physically and positive in his demeanor.

## Chapter 8

# Nicholas Nesterov

## *Red Army Soldier*

During the Great Patriotic War, millions of Red Army soldiers were captured by the enemy but by becoming a prisoner of war each soldier was guilty of violating Order No. 270. The order was dated August 16, 1941 and was signed by Joseph Stalin acting as the People's Commissar of Defense. The first article within the order stated that any military commanders or commissars "tearing away their insignia and deserting or surrendering" should be considered malicious deserters. The order required superiors to shoot the deserters on the spot. Their family members were to be subjected to arrest. The second article demanded that encircled Red Army soldiers must use every possibility to fight on and to demand that their commanders organize the fighting. According to the order, anyone who attempted to surrender instead of fighting must be killed and their family members must be deprived of any State welfare and assistance. Commenting on the order, Stalin declared: "There are no Soviet prisoners of war, only traitors." (see Document Two—Order No.270)

Millions of Soviet prisoners of war were sent back to the Soviet Union after the cessation of hostilities. Upon their arrival in the Soviet Union, they were brought to filtration camps that were run by the NKVD and at the camps they were interrogated for weeks. According to the State, these former prisoners of war had betrayed the Soviet Union by allowing the enemy to capture them. The burden was on these former Red Army soldiers to prove that they were not traitors. Many were found guilty of betraying their country and were either executed at once or sentenced to do hard labor for ten to twenty-five years. They were "enemies of the people." They were assigned to work in coal mines, to do construction work at large industrial sites, to cut timber, to work at fisheries, to work at steel mills or to work at any site where laborers were needed. These men, who had been condemned, were supposed to be grateful to Stalin for sparing their lives.

Nicholas Nesterov was a Red Army soldier who became a prisoner of war after he was captured by the Germans during the Great Patriotic War. He was born in 1921 into an ethnic Finnish family that lived in Krakol, a village which was part of a collective farm within the Kingisepp District in Leningrad Province. On June 22, 1941, he was scheduled to take an oath of allegiance after having attended a military school, but on that day the Germans invaded the Soviet Union. Sometime later, Nicholas was captured by the Germans and he became a prisoner of war. After Finland signed an armistice agreement with the Soviet Union, Nicholas was brought home to be interrogated by the NKVD. The interrogations lasted one full month and the outcome was and continues to be an enigma.

In 2006, Nicholas was asked to talk about the camps in which he was held as a prisoner of war, the methods used by the NKVD when he was interrogated and the life that he lived after the Great Patriotic War. The following paragraphs are the answers that were given by Nicholas to the questions that were asked of him. The answers have been organized into a chronological narrative and inserted within the narrative are comments of explanation by the authors:

I was born in 1921 and received my early education at a school in Krakol, the village where my family lived. I planned to become an accountant but was sent to an educational institution where I was given a cultural education. Following my graduation, the Soviet Union went to war against Finland. [The war is known as the Winter War and it became evident during the war that the Red Army needed competent military oficers. Thus, following the Winter War the regime of Stalin encouraged young men to attend military academies where they were taught and trained to be military commanders.]

Following the Winter War, I attended a military school in western Ukraine. [Ukraine was a republic within the Soviet Union.] The school was called a cavalry school but the name was a façade. It was a school where those who attended studied rocketry, a new area of study. The information to which we, as students, were exposed was top secret and we were not permitted to write down what we learned. We had to memorize all the information. Our period of study lasted five months and it was concluded with a day of ceremony during which each graduate was to take an oath.

The graduation ceremony was scheduled for Sunday, June 22, 1941. The school was located just 40 kilometers [25 miles] from the southwestern border of the Soviet Union. In the early hours of the day, several of us at the school heard the sound of cannonades. [German Army Group South crossed the southwestern border of the Soviet Union at 4:00 A.M. on June 22, 1941.]

There were four platoons that were to take the oath. The men in the first platoon took their oath in the marching square of the school while the men in the three other platoons were waiting to take theirs. Suddenly, there appeared low flying airplanes bearing German insignias. The Soviet commissar who was overseeing the graduation ceremony assured all who were present not to worry. (see Glossary—commisar) "The airplanes are Soviet aircraft," he said. "We are in a border zone and our reconnaissance planes are marked with various kinds of insignias." After the men in the second platoon had taken their place in the marching square to swear their allegiance, four more German airplanes appeared. They flew even lower than the others and they began shooting. Almost all of the men in the second platoon were killed as well as the Soviet commissar. The men in the third and fourth platoons were standing under the trees nearby and they did not suffer any casualties. I was in one of these platoons. The attack on the men of the second platoon was my introduction to war.

It was not until later that we were told that the Soviet Union was at war. The Germans were already in Ternopol Province and we were sent to join a Red Army tank regiment that had been ordered to stop the German advance. When we arrived, we discovered that within the regiment there was utter chaos. The regiment, which consisted of tanks and infantry soldiers, had no communication system and it had no food. The majority of the high ranking military commanders were "German spies who had infiltrated the Red Army. When lower ranking Russian commanders gave orders, they were shot immediately by the higher ranking commanders who were German spies." Because there were no fortifications near the southwestern border of the Soviet Union, the tank regiment was forced to retreat.

Many battles were fought as we retreated and many Red Army soldiers perished or were captured. I fought for about five months. Sometimes I would be assigned to the group that stayed behind so that the others in our subdivision could retreat safely. There were times when the enemy encircled us and we fought our way out of the encirclements to avoid being captured.

I became a prisoner of war after I was wounded in my leg just below the knee. A medical person placed a splint on my leg and I was brought to a local farm house and placed on some hay. Later that night, an old woman came and told me "All your leaders have left; you are alone." I felt abandoned and believed that my short life was coming to an end. I was twenty years old and I dreamed of one day becoming a general. The dream quickly faded when I learned that the farm house to which I had been brought was in a village that had been captured and was being occupied by the Germans. [The Germans captured the village when they encircled Nicholas and his comrades.]

Among the prisoners of war, the Germans sought out Red Army commanders and Soviet commissars. There were Red Army soldiers who would point out to the Germans the Red Army commanders and the commissars. The Red Army soldiers who did this were native Ukrainian soldiers. Many native Ukrainian soldiers believed that the Soviet Union would lose the war. They had been exposed to German leaflets, dropped from the sky, which promised that "Those who are captured and live here [the Republic of Ukraine] will be released immediately to go home." The native Ukrainian soldiers wanted to go home. There were many native Ukrainian soldiers who were traitors.

My fellow prisoners and I thought that our captors would get rid of us by shooting us. Instead they transported us in horse-drawn wagons to some unknown destination. That night we slept on the floor of a Lutheran Church. I believe we were in Poland. After that we were transported to Germany to a place named Witzendorf. There was no prisoner of war camp in Witzendorf so the Germans had us construct our own wooden barracks. I don't think that the Germans had expected to capture so many Red Army soldiers.

One cannot generalize about the guards at the prisoner of war camps. Some guards were kind and others were hard and cruel.

Once, while we were digging dugouts, we were assigned a guard who was a rather old man. I was told that he was a Russian who had immigrated to Germany after 1917. He said something to me and I replied in a rather rough manner. He responded by striking me on the shoulder with the wooden stock of his rifle. I quickly hobbled away and mixed in with the other prisoners.

The guards would beat us if we did not obey. If you remained quiet and worked hard, they left you alone. If you claimed to be ill and said that you could not work, they would beat you. Did I want to work for the Germans? The answer is no. But if I had refused to work, they would have shot me. We were fed but not very well.

I did not try to escape from the camp. The camp was situated in the middle of Germany and I did not know the German language. It was foolish to try and escape. What would I eat if I did try to escape? If I got caught, I would be sent back to the prison camp. If I should get caught trying to escape a second time, I would be shot.

We received reports about the war but most of what we were told was German propaganda. The Germans issued special newspapers written in Russian. The articles were written by German war correspondents who were responsible for misinforming the Russian soldiers in the prisoner of war camps. It was reported in these newspapers that the city of Leningrad had been captured and that Moscow had fallen. In one of the newspapers, I saw a photograph of Stalin's son, Yakov. [Stalin's son had been captured by the Germans.] The only reliable information that we received was given to us by prisoners who had recently arrived in the camp.

In time a new camp was established near our own. The prisoners in the new camp were Russians but they were treated well. They were fed well; they were provided with music and female companionship. The camp was designed to entice Soviet soldiers to join General Andrey Vlasov's Russian Liberation Army. While I was in captivity, I heard that there were Soviet prisoners of war who did join General Vlasov's army and there were Russians who became spies for Germany. I was offered the opportunity to become a Vlasovite but I refused. (see Glossary—Andrey Vlasov)

It was necessary to be discreet when talking to others. We never discussed politics or any government policy. If you desired to live then you did not discuss Stalinism or Hitlerism. I have read that there were secret organizations within the prisoner of war camps during the war. I was not aware of such organizations while I was a prisoner of war. One of our major topics of discussion was food and how to acquire more bread. We were fed but no worse than the prisoners in Stalin's camps. The German guards were not fed any better than the prisoners.

A black market did exist within the camp. Tobacco was exchanged for pieces of bread and sugar was bartered for tobacco. There was no currency in the camp so we only bartered. We never exchanged our clothes because we had no extra clothes to exchange. The Germans provided us with footwear but this was wooden footwear. Thus, when we were brought on foot to a work site we sounded like ten marching brigades.

I was able to earn extra portions of food by drawing portraits for the German guards. As a teenager, I used to draw pictures of dead people lying in coffins. One evening in the camp, I noticed a German guard who was quietly weeping while looking at a small photograph. I approached the guard and asked him what was wrong and why he was weeping. By this time, I had learned a little German and was able to communicate with the guard. "This is my son," he said, showing me the photograph. "He died along the Russian front and this is the only photograph that I have of him." I suggested that he go to a professional photographer and have the photograph enlarged. "Photography," he replied "is prohibited in Germany." The development of photographs was no longer permitted in Germany and Germany's citizens had been ordered to turn in their cameras to the government. I told the guard that if he provided me with paper and a black leaded pencil, I would draw a portrait of his son. "If you give me colored pencils, I will draw a colored portrait." The next day, the guard brought me good paper, a pencil and a large piece of bread. He also arranged it so that I would not be required to work that day. I completed the portrait and when I presented it to the guard, he almost fell down with shock. He liked it so much that he told the other guards about my ability to draw. Some of them brought me photographs of their family members and they also gave me food for the portraits. I earned more than enough food and shared half of it with other prisoners.

My next prison camp was located in Oldenburg, Germany. It consisted of barracks that were made of stone and the bottoms of the beds were made of metal wire netting. It was the best and cleanest of all the prisoner of war camps in which I was detained. They fed us well. We were even given butter with our meals and if they ran out of butter they gave us fruit sweets [these were candied fruits]. The Germans had us unload wood from ships as well as concrete and cement.

Soon after we arrived, the camp was struck by a deadly outbreak of typhus. As many as ten prisoners died each day in spite of the medical care that we were given. The medical care was provided by prisoners who by profession were physicians or veterinarians or who had before the war worked in hospitals as medical assistants. Swedes working for the Red Cross were also brought into the camp. The mattresses were removed and we began sleeping on just the metal netting of the beds but none of the efforts ended the epidemic. The person who became a victim of the disease would bloat up for about three days and then he would die. When we saw a person bloat up, we knew that he would soon pass away. One of the victims was a Russian sailor from Oranianbaum. I had made his acquaintance and he asked me, just before he died, to inform his mother about his death if ever I made it back to Russia. I was immune to typhus because my father had been exposed to the disease before I was born. Those of us who were unaffected by the disease were brought to another camp.

We were transported across the North Sea to Norway which was occupied by the Germans. Our transport began at night after we were loaded onto three freight ships. The ships were spaced about one half kilometer from each other. We traveled all that night and throughout the next day. We did not know where we were headed. Towards evening, three British aircraft appeared and they sank the first ship. I was on the second ship. Four hours later, British aircraft appeared again and the third ship was sunk. The Germans on board our ship probably expected a third attack because they permitted us [the prisoners of war] to come to the top deck of the ship. The British, however, did not reappear and we arrived safely in Oslo.

In Norway we built a landing area for airplanes and we cut down trees. They fed us well because a hungry worker is a poor worker. They provided us with boots and we were permitted to leave the camp grounds after work but were expected to be back at roll call which was conducted in the evening. If a person was not present at roll call, his absence was viewed as an attempt to escape. If a person was absent from roll call a second time, he should expect to be shot. The Germans running the camp had each prisoner sign a sheet of paper which bore the policies enforced in the camp. "If a prisoner tried to escape twice, he would be shot."

After Finland ended its war against the Soviet Union, several of us in the camp began making plans to escape and try to reach Finland. The camp was situated just 20 to 25 kilometers [12 to 15 miles] from Finland's border. There were twelve to fifteen of us. We began by gathering a supply of food that we would need during our escape. In the evenings, during our free time,

I would leave the camp grounds and make my way to a nearby village which was inhabited by Finnish speaking people. I am an ethnic Finn and I speak Izhorian which is very similar to the Finnish language. Thus, I was able to communicate with the people in the village. With their assistance, I drew a map that we were to use in our escape to Finland. We assumed that the people in Finland would not harm us since Finland was no longer an ally of Germany. It took just one day for us to reach Finland.

In Finland we were brought to a prisoner of war camp which held Soviet soldiers who were to be sent back to the Soviet Union. It was autumn of 1944 and the war against Germany would not be over until the following year. We were loaded onto freight cars and there were no guards. We were happy to be going home. We sang and we joked. Just a little beyond Wiborg, the train stopped and we were marched into a detention camp surrounded by forest. It was a make-shift camp made up of barbed wire fencing. This was our new prison camp. From there we were transported by train through the war-torn city of Leningrad and to our next destination which was Tula.

In Tula we were detained in a prison camp run by the NKVD. In the camp there were Soviet Union village elders and policemen who had been arrested for collaborating with the Germans while the enemy occupied their villages. There were also Russians who were charged with spying for the enemy. The camp was an interrogation center and each detainee was interrogated by NKVD agents. The interrogations were conducted at night. A person was usually exposed to three interrogations conducted by three different interrogators every night. The three interrogators would compare the answers that were given by the person they had interrogated in order to determine if that person had told the truth.

I was interrogated for one full month. My interrogators asked me all kinds of questions: How did you become a prisoner of war? Where were you during the war? In what prison camps were you held? Who did you meet in the prison camps? I was shown photographs and asked if I had seen any of the people in the photographs. If I had, where and when had I seen them? The interrogators tried to determine whether or not I was an "enemy of the people." They viewed me as well as the other detainees as betrayers of the Motherland. According to Stalin, we were betrayers. Stalin said there are no prisoners of war; there are only betrayers of the Motherland.

The interrogators who questioned me were calm and methodical. They did not raise their voice. They did not hit the table with their fist. They did not use harsh methods with me. I answered their questions truthfully from the beginning to the end. I had nothing to hide. However, I did not mention my activities as an artist while in the prisoner of war camps. Had I told them about the portraits that I drew for the German guards, I would have been sent to a prison camp for ten years. There were Soviet military commanders who were sent to prison camps for twenty-five years. NKVD interrogators could identify the truth and a lie. I did not lie.

At the end of the interrogations, I was called before a committee. The people in this committee asked me several questions that I answered truthfully. I was then given new documents and told that I was permitted to return home to my native village which had already been liberated by the Red Army. But I had only an old overcoat and some special tickets that I could use to purchase train tickets. I did not want to return home naked and barefooted.

There were mines near Tula and I decided to earn some money working at one of the mines. I was hired as an electrician at one of the better mines. The workers in this mine were fed very well; they were fed canned food that came from the United States.

There was a law in the Soviet Union which stated that workers employed in factories, mines and other enterprises were not to be absent from their work place without permission. A worker who missed work one day, could be sentenced to prison for five to seven years. This happened to a friend and me. We decided to attend a circus. My friend had never been to a circus. We failed to ask permission to be absent from the mine and we were gone the entire day. When we left the circus, we were stopped by a military patrol; they wanted to see our documents. The military patrol knew that miners needed special permission to be absent from work. I was wearing regular shoes but my friend was wearing shoes worn by miners. Seeing my friend's mining shoes, the military patrol took my friend to the patrol office. I accompanied my friend and told the person in charge at the office that if he was going to take away my friend then he should take me as well. Thus, we were both detained in the Tula jail.

In a week we were tried and sentenced to five years without freedom. We were sent to a distribution camp. Representatives from various enterprises would come to the camp in search of workers. One day a representative from a sugar mill arrived in search of five workers and I was one of the five that he chose. I was brought to a three story dormitory where all the non-free workers were housed. The sugar mill was located nearby. The free workers at the mill were permitted to go home at the end of the work day. Non-free workers like me could do as we pleased after work but we had to be back in the dormitory by a set time.

While working at the sugar mill an NKVD officer called me into his office. [There was a special office set aside for the NKVD in the sugar mill which was a State owned State managed enterprise.] He talked to me about the difficulties that the Soviet Union was facing. He said that there were enemies within the country. I told him that I did not agree and said that I would not denounce my friends. I assured him that if I became aware of something that might endanger our country, I would let him know. "Otherwise," I told him,

"I do not want to meet with you on a regular basis." [The NKVD officer wanted Nicholas to inform him about people working in the sugar mill who were anti-Communists and enemies of the State. He wanted Nicholas to be his informer in the sugar mill.] The NKVD officer replied that this was fine. He then told me to sign a form stating that I had met with him in his office but that I would not tell anyone about our meeting. I responded by assuring him that I would not tell anyone about our meeting; however, I would not sign any form. My response angered him and I was told to "get out" of his office. I refused to be his mole in the sugar mill.

When the war [the Great Patriotic War] ended, the law under which I was arrested was cancelled. [It was a wartime law.] All who were arrested under the law were released but the authorities did not want all of us to be released at once. If that was done, production at the sugar mill would drop significantly. They divided us into groups and when one group was released or set free, the workers in that group were replaced with free workers who were usually females. I was placed in the last group to be released; I am sure that the NKVD officer had me placed in the last group. He was punishing me for having rejected his offer.

Following my release, I went in search of my parents. I was told by my uncle Ivan, my father's brother, that the people in our village [it was a village populated by ethnic Finns] had been evacuated to Finland by the Germans in late 1943. After Finland signed an armistice agreement with the Soviet Union, my parents and the other people of our village were returned to the Soviet Union but not to our village. They were brought to Kalinin Province. I traveled to Kalinin Province and found my parents working on a collective farm. Because my parents were ethnic Finns, they were not permitted to return to their native village in Leningrad Province. They had lived in Finland during the war and consequently they were not to be trusted as Soviet citizens.

Good fortune smiled on us. Back in 1941, before the Germans arrived in our area [the Kingisepp District of Leningrad Province], my parents were given permission by the authorities to move to Kalinin Province. But my parents never moved to Kalinin Province. However, my father kept the documents giving my parents permission to move to Kalinin Province. When my parents were evacuated by the Germans to Finland in 1943, father took the documents with him. That was fortunate. I took the documents to the regional commissar of the local police and showed him the documents. I did not mention that my parents had been evacuated to Finland during the war. The commissar assumed that my parents had arrived in Kalinin Province back in 1941 and the documents indicated that. Thus, he gave me permission to take my parents back to our native village. He assumed that my parents had not lived under German rule.

After bringing my parents home to our native village, I moved to Leningrad to work as an electrician and to attend school. I attended evening classes, graduated from the tenth grade and entered a vocational school for electricians. Soon thereafter, the director of the school called me into his office and asked me how I had gained admission to his school. I told him that I passed the entrance examination with the highest grades. "But you were a prisoner of war" he said. "Yes," I replied, "I was captured and I wrote that on the application for admission." "But Stalin," he said, "does not allow people who have lived in captivity to attend educational institutions of higher learning or vocational schools." The director then told me that I was no longer permitted to attend his school.

I spent the next twelve years working as an electrician on the country's railways. During that time, I sensed that I was being watched. My senses did not deceive me. The man with whom I was sharing an apartment informed me during a friendly conversation that he had been ordered to spy on me. He told me that he had signed a document which stated that he would not tell anyone about his spying activities. He said that if the authorities should find out that he had confided in me, he would be arrested and sent to prison for ten years. I told him not to worry. "Why would I tell anyone?" I replied. Then he added that there was another person who was also watching me but he did not know who it was. "I will find him myself," I replied, and I did. I told the second spy that I knew that he was watching me and I said to him "When you report to your masters tell them that you are an incompetent spy." A month later, Stalin died.

My life improved after Stalin died. I was hired by an enterprise which produced alcohol that was used to make vodka and medicines. I worked there for many years and was awarded with the Order of the Red Banner of Labor. I attended evening classes at a vocational school that specialized in radio and television repairs. I was even elected as a deputy to the District Council. At the age of fifty-five, I retired from my job and now I enjoy a comfortable lifestyle on my monthly pension.

On my passport it states that I am a Russian. I am Chukhua [an ethnic Finn] but I remain silent about my nationality. My last name is Russian and since ancient times my ancestors have worshipped as Russian Orthodox Christians. If someone should ask me what it was that helped me survive the war, I will tell that person it was good luck and nothing more. As an electrician, I was electrocuted four times. Yet I survived. I was just lucky.

*Chapter 9*

# Mikhail Zoshchenko and Anna Akhmatova

## *Enemies of the People?*

In 1946 Stalin initiated a campaign against all attitudes that he considered harmful to Soviet values. The campaign was entrusted to Andrei Zhdanov, a Politburo member and the Commissar for Culture. The campaign, which was later named Zhdanovshchina (Zhdanov's reign), consisted of measures that were designed to purge anti-Soviet elements and decadent Western influences from literature, art and music. The fine arts, it was decided, must serve the purposes of Marxism, Leninism and Stalinism, and should be so crafted that they would instill within Soviet citizens national patriotism.

The starting point of the campaign was the city of Leningrad when on August 14, 1946, the Central Committee of the Russian Communist Party issued a decree censoring two literary journals, *Zvezda* (The Star) and *Leningrad,* for publishing the "debased" works of two Leningrad writers, Mikhail Zoshchenko and Anna Akhmatova. Zoshchenko was a satirist and Stalin had long been irritated by his stories. Especially annoying was Zoshchenko's *Adventures of a Monkey* published in 1946. It was a satire about a monkey who escaped from a zoo during the war.

Zhdanov denounced the short story with the following comments:

If you will read that story carefully and think it over, you will see that Zoshchenko casts the monkey in the role of the supreme judge of our social order. . . . The monkey is presented as a kind of rational principle having the right to evaluate the conduct of human beings. The picture of Soviet life is deliberately and vilely distorted and caricatured so that Zoshchenko can put into the mouth of his monkey a vile, poisonous anti-Soviet sentiment to the effect that life is better in the zoo than at liberty and that one breathes more easily in a cage than among Soviet people. Is it possible to sink to a lower political and moral level? And how could the Leningraders endure to publish in their journals such fifth and nonsense?[1]

Zoshchenko's work, Zhdanov concluded, was "a vile obscenity." It violated the doctrine of Socialist Realism which demanded that the various forms of fine art, such as literature, must depict some aspect of the human struggle toward socialist progress for a better life. According to Zhdanov, the outstanding heroes of literary works are those who portray "real" life and whose main characters are optimistic and heroic. At the same time, their written works will educate the masses in socialism and more specifically Marxian socialism.

The themes in literature were to emphasize the importance and beauty of work and the successes of Stalin's five-year-plans. The factory workers and the agricultural workers in the collective farms were elevated by presenting their labor as admirable. Tragedy and negativity were not permitted unless they were used to describe a different time or place. Writers were not to describe life just as they saw it because anything that reflected poorly on Marxian socialism or on Stalin and the decisions made by the leadership of the Russian Communist Party had to be omitted. Thus, authors had to describe a reality which did not actually exist.

The official denunciation of Zoshchenko was quickly translated into action. Zoshchenko was expelled from the Union of Soviet Writers. (see Glossary—Union of Soviet Writers) Barred from publication, Zoshchenko was forced to work as a translator and resume his first career as a shoemaker. Following Stalin's death in 1953, he was readmitted to the Union of Soviet Writers. But by this time, Zoshchenko had fallen into such a deep depression that he produced no major writings before his death in 1958.

Anna Akhmatova like Zoshchenko would not promote Socialist Realism. She was born Anna Anreyevna Gorenko in 1889 near the city of Odessa, Ukraine in Tsarist Russia. Her interest in poetry began in her youth but when her father learned about her aspirations, he told her not to shame the family name by becoming a "decadent poetess." He forced her to take a pen name and she chose the last name of her maternal great-grandmother. She attended law school in Kiev and in 1910 married Nikolai Gumilev who was a poet and literary critic. Shortly after their marriage, Nikolai traveled to Abyssinia leaving Anna behind. While Nikolai was away, Anna wrote many of the poems that would be included in her first book entitled *Vecher* (Evening) published in 1912. In this same year, Anna gave birth to her son who was named Lev.

Anna's second book of poems entitled *Chetki* (Rosary) was published in 1914. It was critically acclaimed and brought her fame within the literary community of St. Petersburg.

During World War One and during the early years of Bolshevik (Communist) rule in Russia, Anna produced civic, patriotic and religious collections such as *Belaya Staya* (The White Flock) published in 1917, *Podorozhnik* (Plantain) published 1921 and *Anno Domini MCMXXI* published in 1922. The Bolshevik (Communist) leadership criticized Anna's work, identifying it as "bourgeois and aristocratic" and they condemned it for Anna's preoccupation with love and God.

Anna's life as a publicly recognized poet was further complicated after Nikolai, who disdained the Bolshevik government, was arrested, tried and executed by the Cheka in 1921. (see Glossary—NKVD) He was accused of participating in an anti-Soviet conspiracy. It was a trumped-up charge. Although Anna and Nikolai were no longer married to each other (Anna had divorced Nikolai in 1918), she was still identified with her former husband, an "enemy of the people." Consequently, Anna would be viewed with suspicion by the State authorities who made her life increasingly difficult. (In 1918, Anna married Vladimir Shileiko whom she divorced in 1928 and then she lived with Nikolai Punin who died in a Siberian prison labor camp in 1953.)

Following the publication of *Anno Domini MCMXXI*, Anna entered a period of almost complete silence and literary ostracism. No volume of her poetry would be published in the Soviet Union until 1940.

In 1940 a collection of previously published poems, titled *From Six Books,* was published. But a few months later, the volume was withdrawn. Apparently, she was still viewed and condemned by the State authorities as a "bourgeois element."

During Anna's forced silence (1922–1940), she researched the life and works of Alexander Pushkin whom she admired as a poet and who had lived in St. Petersburg 100 years earlier. Her scholarly articles concerning Pushkin were published posthumously under the title *On Pushkin*. In order to earn money, Anna worked as a critic and translator, producing Russian versions of works by Victor Hugo and Giacomo Leopardi and others. Nevertheless, money was desperately short and she lived in poverty. Anna also found it difficult to obtain a proper education for her son because institutions of education were unwilling to accept a child that was marked as "anti-Soviet" by association. Lev's father had been executed as an "enemy of the people."

The 1930s were especially difficult for Anna. A number of her friends became victims of Stalin's purges. At the same time, as it was later revealed, Anna was under constant government surveillance and a dossier of denunciations was being compiled. Then in 1935, Lev and Nikolai Punin, Anna's common law husband, were arrested and charged with political deviance. Both were soon released but Lev was arrested again in 1938 and subsequently served a five-year sentence in the Gulag. He was identified as an "enemy of the people" and Anna was recognized as the mother of an "enemy of the people."

In response to the accumulation of horrors that Anna endured, she composed between 1935 and 1940 a sequence of poems titled *Requiem*. In them she describes her anguish over her son's imprisonment. She also recounts the sufferings of other Soviet citizens living under Stalinism. More specifically, she was able to empathize with the wives and mothers with whom she stood in line outside the walls of the prisons where their husbands and sons were being detained, awaiting to be tried. In the great majority of cases, the victims were sentenced to do hard labor for several years in a prison camp located somewhere in Siberia. The women hoped to get one last glimpse of their loved ones before they were transported out and exiled.

The following stanzas are English translations of Anna's *Requiem*:

> During the frightening years of the [Nikolai] Yezhov terror, I
> spent seventeen months waiting in prison queues in
> Leningrad. One day, somehow someone 'picked me out.'
> On that occasion there was a woman standing behind me,
> her lips blue with cold, who, of course, had never in
> her life heard my name. Jolted out of the torpor
> characteristic of all of us, she said into my ear
> (everyone whispered there)—'Could one ever describe
> this?' And I answered—'I can.' It was then that
> something like a smile slid across what had previously
> been just a face.
> [added on the 1st of April in the year 1957, Leningrad]
> INTRODUCTION
> [PRELUDE]
> It happened like this when only the dead
> Were smiling, glad of their release,
> That Leningrad hung around its prisons
> Like a worthless emblem, flapping its piece.
> Shrill and sharp, the steam-whistles sang
> Short songs of farewell
> To the ranks of convicted, demented by suffering,
> As they, in regiments, walked along-
> Stars of death stood over us
> As innocent Russia squirmed
> Under the blood-spattered boots and tires
> Of the Black Marias [Black Ravens].
> I
> You were taken away at dawn. I followed you
> As one does when a corpse is being removed.
> Children were crying in the darkened house.

A candle flared, illuminating the Mother of God . . .
The cold of an icon was on your lips, a death-cold sweat
On your brow—I will never forget this; I will gather
To wail with the wives of the murdered streltsy
Inconsolably, beneath the Kremlin towers.
[written in Autumn, 1935 in Moscow]
II
Silent flows the river Don
A yellow moon looks quietly on
Swanking about, with cap askew
It sees through the window a shadow of you
Gravely ill, all alone
The moon sees a woman lying at home
Her son is in jail, her husband is dead
Say a prayer for her instead.
IV
Giggling, poking fun, everyone's darling,
The carefree sinner of Tsarskoye Selo
If only you could have foreseen
What life would do with you —
That you would stand, parcel in hand,
Beneath the Crosses, three hundred in line,
Burning the new year's ice
With your hot tears.
Back and forth the prison poplar sways
With not a sound—how many innocent
Blameless lives are being taken away . . .
[written in 1938]
V
For seventeen months I have been screaming,
Calling you home.
I've thrown myself at the feet of butchers [State authorities]
For you, my son [Lev] and my horror.
Everything has become muddled forever —
I can no longer distinguish
Who is an animal, who a person, and how long
The wait can be for an execution.
There are now only dusty flowers,
The chinking of the thurible,
Tracks from somewhere into nowhere.
And, staring me in the face
And threatening me with swift annihilation,
An enormous star [the red star symbolizing the Soviet Union].
[written in 1939]
VII

THE VERDICT
The word landed with a stony thud
Onto my still-beating breast.
Never mind, I was prepared,
I will manage with the rest.
I have a lot of work to do today.
I need to slaughter memory,
Turn my living soul to stone
Then teach myself to live again . . .
But how. The hot summer rustles
Like a carnival outside my window.
I have long had this premonition
Of a bright day and a deserted house.
[written 22 June 1939 at Fontannyi Dom]
VIII
TO DEATH
You will come anyway—so why not now?
I wait for you; things have become too hard.
I have turned out the lights and opened the door
For you, so simple and so wonderful.
Assume whatever shape you wish. Burst in
Like a shell of noxious gas. Creep up on me
Like a practiced bandit with a heavy weapon.
Poison me, if you want, with a typhoid exhalation,
Or, with a simple tale prepared by you
(And known by all to the point of nausea), take me
Before the commander of the blue caps and let me glimpse
The house administrator's terrified white face.
I don't care anymore. The river Yenisey
Swirls on. The Pole star blazes.
The blue sparks of those much-loved eyes
Close over and cover the final horror.
[written in August 1939 at Fontannyi Dom]
X
CRUCIFIXION
Weep not for me, mother
I am alive in my grave.
1.
A choir of angels glorified the greatest hour,
The heavens melted into flames.
To his father he said, 'Why hast thou forsaken me!'
But to his mother, 'Weep not for me . . . '
[written in 1940 at Fontannyi Dom]
2.
Magdalena smote herself and wept,

The favorite disciple turned to stone,
But there, where the mother stood silent,
Not one person dared to look.
[written in 1943in Tashkent]
EPILOGUE
1.
I have learned how faces fall,
How terror can escape from lowered eyes,
How suffering can etch cruel pages
Of cuneiform-like marks upon the cheeks.
I know how dark or ash-blond strands of hair
Can suddenly turn white. I've learned to recognize
The fading smiles upon submissive lips,
The trembling fear inside a hollow laugh.
That's why I pray not for myself
But all of you who stood there with me
Through fiercest cold and scorching July heat
Under a towering, completely blind red wall [prison wall].
2.
The hour has come to remember the dead.
I see you, I hear you, I feel you:
The one who resisted the long drag to the open window.
The one who could no longer feel the kick of familiar soil beneath
her feet.
The one who, with a sudden flick of her head, replied,
'I arrive here as if I've come home!'
I'd like to name you all by name, but the list
Has been removed and there is nowhere to look.
So,
I have woven you this wide shroud out of the humble words
I overhear you use. Everywhere, forever and always,
I will never forget one single thing. Even in new grief.
Even if they clamp shut my tormented mouth
Through which one hundred million people scream.
That's how I wish them to remember me when I am dead
On the eve of my remembrance day.
If someone someday in this country
Decides to raise a memorial to me,
I give my consent to this festivity
But only on this condition—do not build it
By the sea where I was born,
I have severed my last ties with the sea;
Nor in the Tsar's Park by the hallowed stump
Where an inconsolable shadow looks for me;
Build it here where I stood for three hundred hours

And no-one slid open the bolt [prison cell door].
Listen, even in blissful death I fear
That I will forget the Black Marias [Black Ravens],
Forget how hatefully the door slammed and an old woman
Howled like a wounded beast.
Let the thawing ice flow like tears
From my immovable bronze eyelids
And let the prison dove coo in the distance
While ships sail quietly along the river.

*Requiem* is considered Anna's most accomplished work.

After Hitler's Germany invaded the Soviet Union in 1941, Anna was permitted by the State authorities to deliver an inspiring radio address to the women of Leningrad. After the Germans with their allies, the Finns, established a blockade against the city of Leningrad, the authorities ordered Anna to be flown out of the city over the German front lines and to Moscow. From there she was brought to Tashkent, Uzbekistan, out of harm's way, where she spent the rest of the war years. To assist in the war effort, Anna would visit the hospitalized Soviet soldiers who were brought to Tashkent and she would read to them her poems. A small volume of selected poems was published in Tashkent in 1943 and at the end of the war (the Great Patriotic War) she returned to Leningrad where her poems began to appear in local magazines and newspapers. She gave poetic readings and plans were made for the publication of a large edition of her works.

But in August 1946, Anna was denounced by the Central Committee of the Russian Communist Party for her "eroticism, mysticism and political indifference." Her poetry was castigated as "alien to the Soviet people" and she was publicly insulted by Andrey Zhdanov. He claimed that her poetry was "empty, inane. . . . Her verse, nourished in the spirit of pessimism and decadence . . . cannot be tolerated in Soviet literature." Zhdanov wrote that "[her] subject matter is throughout individualist. The range of her poetry is pathetically limited. It is the poetry of a half-crazy gentile lady, who tosses back and forth between the bedroom and the chapel. . . . Half nun and half harlot, or rather both nun and harlot, her harlotry is mingled with prayer."[2]

Then in 1950, a number of Anna's poems eulogizing Stalin and Soviet communism were printed in several issues of a weekly magazine *Ogonyok* (The Little light) under the title *Iz tsikla "Slava mirn"* (From the Cycle "Glory to Peace"). In one of the poems, Akhmatova declares that "Where Stalin is, there is freedom, peace and the grandeur of the earth." It was obvious that Akhmatova wanted to propitiate Stalin and thus win the freedom of her son who, in 1949, had been arrested again. Lev was accused of being involved in an anti-Soviet group and was sentenced to ten years in a prison labor camp in Siberia. Anna's actions however, did not win Lev's release.

After the death of Stalin in 1953, Anna was permitted to publish her poetry again. In 1958 Anna's *Poems* was published followed by *Poems: 1909–1960* published in 1961. The *Requiem* was published in the Soviet Union for the first time in 1989, twenty-three years after Anna's death. She died in Leningrad where she had lived for a great part of her life.

## NOTES

1. Edward J. Brown, *Russian Literature since the Revolution* (Cambridge, Massachusetts: Harvard University Press, 1982), 226–27.

2. Brown, *Russian Literature since the Revolution*, 227.

## Chapter 10

# Nila Shevko

## *Exiled to Siberia*

Nila Shevko[1] was a Soviet citizen whose life was impacted strongly by Stalinism. She spent her early childhood in Dursk in Central Russia and when she became an adult she moved to Moscow and supported herself working at a variety of jobs. In Moscow she would meet her future husband, Karel Gahlin. Nila was not politically active but Karel joined the Oppositionists and worked to get Stalin removed from power. Karel was arrested by the NKVD and was sentenced into exile to Siberia. (see Glossary—NKVD) From then on Nila was identified as the wife of an "enemy of the people." She would no longer be addressed in public as "Comrade" but as "Citizen." Nila visited her husband in Siberia and assisted him and his friends who had started an opposition movement in the community of Chita.

Upon Nila's return to Moscow, she was arrested by the NKVD and was detained in the Lubyanka, the most famous prison in Moscow. Nila was an unconventional, independent minded, spirited young woman. She would make demands and oppose prison rules. She would be transferred from Lubyanka to the Butirki Prison where, for several months, she would be placed in solitary confinement in the Tower of Pugachev. From there she would be transported to Sverdlovsk Prison and finally she would be brought to a village named Tabov located near the Arctic Circle. Upon her arrival in Tabov, she discovered that the village was policed by an NKVD officer. He would eventually send Nila back to Moscow under the escort of two NKVD men.

When Nila arrived in Tyumen, she was informed by an NKVD officer that the most important Oppositionists had decided to end their opposition towards Stalin and that her husband had left the Opposition movement. It was in Tyumen where Nila was reunited with her husband who had been released from prison. Both Nila and her husband would return to Moscow and both would be given employment for five years.

In December 1934, Sergei Kirov, one of Stalin's important lieutenants, was assassinated in the city of Leningrad. Stalin used the murder to liquidate the Oppositionists and what followed was the Great Purge. Most everybody who had ever opposed Stalin was arrested. Karel was among the thousands who were arrested by the NKVD. He was exiled to a prison work camp in Kolyma.

The following paragraphs contain Nila's recollections which begin with her birth and end with her leaving Moscow after her second husband, Robert Magidoff, was accused by the Soviet government of being an American spy. Both Nila and Robert were brought to the United States and freedom following the Great Patriotic War (World War Two).

## NILA'S ACCOUNT

I was born in the village of Devinishki in Byelorussia in November 1905. At first everybody thought that I would not live long because I was born ill. I was so sick that my father, whose name was Ivan Shevko, and my mother, Maria Ivanovna or simply Marya, decided not to christen me until they were sure that I was going to live. Christening was expensive, costing from five to ten rubles. My parents decided that it was foolish to spend the money "if the child is not going to survive." My parents were not uncaring. Life was not easy and they had to be careful not to squander their money.

After waiting another month, they decided that they would have me christened but they had not yet decided on a name for me. My mother had a sister, Liza, who was considered to be somewhat strange. She was the black pig [black sheep] of the family. She always dreamed of traveling to faraway places and she would often read poetry after she returned from working in the fields. My aunt Liza chose my name, Neonila, which was the name of a great sinner in an old Russian book. Aunt Liza thought that this was a fine name.

In tsarist Russia when a child was brought to be christened, the child was given one of the names identified with the date of the christening in the Russian Orthodox Church. It was winter and the priest, dressed in a big fur coat, a cap and gloves, refused at first to christen me with the name Neonila. I had to be given a proper name, he said. But after a while he was so terribly cold that he decided to christen me no matter what name for me was chosen. Then, using my legs to break the ice that had formed in his water basin, the priest submerged my naked body in the ice-cold water three times [in the name of God the Father, God the Son and God the Holy Spirit].

My mother believed that this was the end for me. Before the priest submerged me, I was making weak little noises but after the christening, I made no noise. All day long, after we returned home, I exhibited no sign of life. Russian peasants, my parents were peasants, were not afraid to joke about death. So, mother and her friends discussed whether to make me a dress to be buried in or not. Then they heard me cry and I would never be a sick baby again.

I was the second child in the family. I had an older brother named Nikolai and later on two sisters, Alexandra and Zinaida.

One of the strongest memories of my childhood was watching my father pray. He would stand facing one of the corners inside the house and pray and pray. However, I never considered him a religious man. He just made the sign of the cross and murmured the prayers mechanically. I never saw my mother pray but she had a deeply religious soul and we children sensed it because of her saintly goodness.

My father was a rude man. He was big and grew a big black mustache. His job was taking care of horses and cleaning stables. He was the type of husband who expected to be treated as the tsar of the family since he was the family's provider.

In the evenings he would come home and sit down at the table to eat. He would never say what he wanted. It was beneath his dignity to ask for a spoon or some salt or some bread. My mother was expected to guess what he wanted. I never heard the words "thank you" used by my family.

I was a very ugly child. I was strangely built. My arms were so long that my hands almost came down to my knees. I looked like a gorilla. One day, when I was seven years old, I heard my mother say to a neighbor woman "When I look at that child, I am so worried because nobody will ever marry her." Mother was not being cruel. Mother was born into a hard and simple cultural environment and she believed that for a woman to survive, she must be married. Thus, every night I prayed that God would send me a husband, even a one-legged husband. My mother's concern caused me to worry that I might never be married.

When I was seven and a half, I was sent to live with one of my grandmothers. There were too many mouths to feed at home. Many years later, I asked mother why I was chosen to live with my grandmother. Mother replied that I was the kind of person who had the ability to adjust to change.

I hated living with grandmother. She, like so many Russian peasant women, expressed no gentleness. She would say hurtful things. One day, I became so angry with her that I went to the rear of the house and with some matches lighted the roof which was made of straw. One corner of the house was burned before someone was able to put out the fire. The incident did not improve my relationship with grandmother and she continued to make hurtful remarks. She would often criticize me claiming that I was not dependable. There were times when she would beat me.

I finally decided to kill myself because I couldn't stand my life anymore. I had heard my grandmother talking about a farm girl who had committed suicide. The girl had taken a box of matches, dissolved the match heads in water and then she drank the solution. So, I took some matches and dissolved the ends in water. Because the farm girl had left a note to her boyfriend, I also left a note informing my grandmother that because of her, I was killing myself. But I didn't die. I swallowed just enough of the solution to get sick and then I vomited. When grandmother discovered what I had done, she had me drink lots of milk and then she put me to bed. However, the incident did not persuade grandmother to change her attitude towards me; she did not soften.

It was Easter when grandmother told my mother, who was visiting, that she no longer wanted me living with her. Thereafter, mother sent me to live with an aunt who was a teacher in a village school. The entire school building consisted of two rooms. One room was my aunt's living quarters and the other was the school classroom. Being the teacher's niece went to my head. I was snobbish towards the other students as if I was aristocracy. I made up stories about how my family lived and what kind of food we ate. I had read stories about the aristocracy in books and they became my sources of information.

My aunt sent me back to mother but by this time my family had moved to the city of Kursk in Central Russia. So, mother applied and got me registered into a school for orphans and for girls of poor families. The school was located in Kursk under the fund of Queen Mother, Maria Feodorovna.

When I arrived at the school, I was given an ugly uniform made of gray cotton. We were called the Gray Girls. Gray is not just a color in Russia, it also implies backwardness. The uniform consisted of a long skirt which reached down to the ankles and it had a round cape-like collar. Our hair was cut short and we wore heavy uncomfortable boots with buttons. There was nothing feminine about our apparel. I was the most unpresentable creature. I was ten years old, wild, disorganized and uncoordinated.

At the age of twelve, the Bolshevik Revolution [October Revolution] broke out. Russia had already been at war for three years [World War One]. I didn't know much about the war and I knew absolutely nothing about the Bolshevik Revolution. My first glimpse of the revolution was when I saw soldiers marching with little red bows on their rifles. I asked my supervisor about the red bows but she did not want to talk about the revolution. She said the soldiers were a bunch of drunkards who decided to put bows on their rifles. Shortly thereafter, the orphan school was closed because it was a tsarist institution. Thus, I went back to my family.

The Bolshevik Revolution was followed by a civil war between the White Army and the Red Army. During the war, control over the city of Kursk changed hands several times. You would wake up in the morning not knowing which side controlled the city. A woman did not know if she should wear a red button which would mean that she supported the Bolsheviks [the Reds] or if she should hang a small cross from a chain around her neck indicating that she supported the Whites.

Life was hard and mother became involved in various enterprises in order to support and feed the family. During a time when the White Army controlled the city, mother would make potato pancakes and sell them at the railroad station. She would boil whole potatoes that were unpeeled, flatten them into round cakes and then fry them in oil pressed from sunflower seeds. She would place the potato cakes in a dish and cover the dish in a pillow to keep the cakes warm. When the trains arrived, mother and I would go to the railroad station and yell "Hot pancakes! Hot pancakes!"

The family's situation began to improve after my brother got a job working in a flour mill. He would get paid two pounds of wheat flour for one day of work. I remember how proud he was on the day he brought home the first two pounds of flour. As a family, we did not need all of the flour, so mother began making pancakes using the extra flour.

Our situation continued to improve after father got a job guarding the freight cars while they were parked at the railroad station. At this time hooliganism and vandalism existed everywhere in revolutionary Russia. Hooliganism and vandalism are products of two states of existence. A person is either so rich that out of boredom he goes out and breaks things or he is so poor that he resorts to stealing in order to survive. In revolutionary Russia, people would steal that which would help them survive. That is why father was hired to guard the freight cars when they were parked at the railroad station. As payment, father would be given either sunflower oil or salt. One day father brought home ten pounds of salt and we were thrilled. Salt was expensive and it was in demand. We exchanged a portion of the salt for bread, butter and cottage cheese.

Because life was so hard, the government felt that it was necessary to give the people something that would make life more pleasant. They gave us organized dances. The entire country went wild with this new pastime. After every show or movie in a theater, there would be an hour of dancing. In every factory, the workers, after a day's work, would spend some time dancing with each other. Prior to the Bolshevik Revolution, dancing was an activity in which only the nobility participated. But now the working masses, the proletariat, adopted this activity of entertainment. Everyone was dancing waltzes and mazurkas. [A mazurka is a Polish folk dance.] The directors of the dances usually spoke in French, not in Russian. The French language was considered more elegant.

There were contests where a dancing couple could win a prize. The prizes were usually practical items such as two pounds of sugar, five pounds of salt, a big loaf of good black bread or some sunflower oil. Father always knew where the dancing contests were being held but he never understood the pleasure of dancing. He was interested in the prizes and he would urge my brother and me to participate in the contests.

My brother was an excellent dancer and he and I won a number of contests. The prizes that we won, plus my father's job and my brother's employment helped make life for my family less difficult.


## Nila Moves to Moscow

Everybody in Russia wanted to live in Moscow and so did I. So, when I was eighteen years old, I traveled to Moscow alone in a railroad cattle car. Mother was very much against my going. "How will you support yourself?" she asked. "I don't know," I answered truthfully, "but I will do something."

During my first day in Moscow, I walked up and down the streets in search of a place to stay. While looking, I saw an old woman, carrying two big bundles, fall to the ground. I rushed to help her up and together we walked to where she lived. Her name was Matryona. She wanted to make me a cup of tea but when I told her that I would rather have a place to live, she suggested organizing a bed for me in the corridor of the house where she lived. It was the corridor that was used by everyone who lived in the house. I agreed and in order to give me a degree of privacy, Matryona hung some green curtains around the mattress. This is where I lived for one year.

In Moscow, I found work at the very famous Agricultural Exposition. It was the first large exposition that the Soviets organized. They wanted to use the exposition to impress the world with their agricultural achievements. I was given a job washing the floor in the pavilion. I did my job well and was promoted. I checked the tickets of the people who visited the exposition. Every day I checked the tickets and every day a Red Army soldier, whose name was Grisha, was there with me to make sure that nothing was stolen.

One afternoon there appeared a beautifully dressed woman with a large hat accompanied by a man with a long beard. The woman was holding in her hand a beautiful bouquet of flowers that had been on display at the exposition. As they were about to leave, I asked her politely for a pass which gave her permission to take the flowers. You see, nobody was permitted to leave the exposition with flowers or bundles or anything without a pass. My demand to see a pass angered the bearded man who accompanied her and he pushed me aside with his arm. I reacted in anger and told Grisha, who was on duty, to arrest them both.

Grisha arrested them and escorted them with his rifle through the length of the exposition to the main entrance which was where the offices were located. Upon their arrival, there followed complete confusion. The bearded man was the Vice-Commissar of Justice of the Soviet Republics. His name was Beloborodov, which means "white-bearded one." Grisha was removed from his post and was arrested.

After I returned home, I told Mytryona what had happened at the exposition. I told her that soon I too would be arrested and probably executed. Immediately Granny, which is what I called Mytryona, started to bake a loaf of bread that I could take with me to prison should I be arrested. It was customary for relatives and friends to come to prison and bring with them packages of food for a prisoner. There is a special name in Russia for such a package—*peredatcha*.

The next day a military man appeared at the door and walked me to Lubyanka. Everything that is terrible could be found in that building such as the offices of the secret police and their prisons. The name Lubyanka struck terror in the minds of Russians because it was a most horrifying place.

When we got there, I saw Grisha sitting without his belt or his rifle. They had taken everything away from him. "Nila, what will happen to us?" he asked. "I don't know," I answered, "we were only doing our job."

I was taken into a long, beautiful room and brought before the Head Commissar, Comrade Krylenko, and seven or eight other men, including Beloborodov. They were seated around a long conference table. I was ushered to the end of the table and there I stood in a straight cut dress with no form or shape, without a belt, without shoes and with a short haircut. "Do you know this man?" the Head Commissar asked pointing to Beloborodov. "Yes," I answered. Then Beloborodov was told to tell his account of what happened at the exposition. Beloborodov gave his account and went on and on describing my actions and how awfully I behaved.

Then it was my turn. I stood straight and motionless with both arms close to my side like a soldier at inspection and I told them what had happened. Very calmly I said, "Comrade Beloborodov, you are lying." There was complete silence in the room. Everyone knew the seriousness of my remark. It could result in my execution. I continued, explaining that all I did was to ask politely to see the pass for the flowers that were in the hands of the beautifully dressed woman who was with Beloborodov. "He got angry and pushed me aside," I explained, "but I was only doing my job."

The most unbelievable events then happened. The Head Commissar stood up and walked around the table, put his hands on my shoulders and said, "If everybody, Comrade Shevko, will be as honest as you are and not be afraid to fight for his rights, the Soviet Republics will be as strong as can be. I am proud to be a citizen of the same country as you." Then he leaned down and kissed me.

"I will not be shot?" I asked, in unbelief.

"Certainly not. Go and work and do your duty for the Republic."

Then the Head Commissar turned to Beloborodov and scolded him saying, "I am ashamed of you! I am ashamed of you! I am ashamed of you!"

Grisha and I rode back to the Agricultural Exposition in the Head Commissar's automobile. It was really something. Never before had I ridden in an automobile and here I was going through Moscow in this big black automobile with a chauffeur. I do not know what kind of an automobile it was, maybe a Packard or a Cadillac. I knew nothing about automobiles at that time; nevertheless, it was terrific.

At the exposition, Grisha and I were given a month's salary and they gave me a raincoat and a pair of shoes. They also wrote a very patriotic story about the incident and submitted it to the newspaper. Thereafter, when people visiting the exposition were shown around by the guards, the guards would say, "Here is wheat and here is the young woman who arrested the Vice-Commissar."

When the agriculture exposition came to an end, the officials gave me ten pounds of sugar and a train ticket back to Kursk. I went home believing that I was a hero, an absolute hero.

After a short while in Kursk, I returned to Moscow and found a job as a packer in a tea factory named Red Rose. The tea was imported from China in large bundles and as soon as it arrived it was placed on electric conveyers for the workers to package.

Initially, I loved the job because the Chinese put presents in with the tea. They were charming items such as aluminum rings, knives, little dolls and little statues of gods. As we worked, we were being watched by an NKVD officer. (see Glossary—NKVD) The government in Moscow was concerned that the Chinese might send anti-Soviet propaganda. Thus, if the NKVD man saw anything written in Chinese, he would immediately confiscate it.

The managers at the factory were constantly pushing us to work faster. They would take a group of employees who worked very fast and would use that group's work production quota as the new quota that every group had to meet. It was physically impossible and so I helped organize a sit-down strike. Those who participated in the strike, including myself, were fired.

## Nila Meets Karel

It was during one of the meetings at which the sit-down strike was being organized that I met a handsome man named Karl Gahlin. Everybody called him Karel. He was born into a highly educated and cultured family. His father had a college education and Karel was also educated. He was a poet and was very active in the youth movement. He and his friends expressed themselves beautifully using German and French phrases. One of Karel's favorite writers was Marcel Proust. But Karel was also a crazy man. He had revolutionary ideas and did not believe in being nicely dressed. If a hole appeared in the heel of one of his socks, he would wear it so that the hole would show.

I do not know what he saw in me that attracted him. I was very homely. My hair was cut short and at that time in Russia no woman had her hair done in a permanent. When I first heard the word permanent used in Russia, the word permanent sounded like a curse word. "You permanent!"

I used to ask Karel "What is it about me that you love?" I told him that I was a simple peasant woman. "I am a baba," I told him. A baba is someone who is ignorant and stupid, someone who is not good looking, someone who has not been raised with etiquette and with manners and someone who has no standing in society. One day Karel answered, "I don't understand it myself." Still Karel courted me heavily and finally I married him.

Karel was a member of the Russian Communist Party and the Party sent him to the city of Leningrad to work as an editor at the publishing house. I went to Leningrad with Karel. I was not a member of the Party and I had no job waiting for me. So, I went to the employment bureau in Leningrad and the workers there found me a job in a factory that made doors and windows and wooden parts for railroad cars.

Later Karel was assigned to work in Khabarovsk, the capital of Far East Russia. I accompanied him and in time I got a job working in the employment bureau of the Commissariat of Supply. I was the person to whom people would go to register for a job. I would give a person a form to complete and then take the completed form to the NKVD for them to check and determine if the applicant should or should not be hired. Everybody in the Soviet Union seeking employment was checked by the NKVD. People who had a checkered past or who had family members who were capitalists, or who had been arrested and exiled were denied employment. The NKVD office was located a distance from our office, so I was provided with a horse and a two wheeled cart to go forth and back.

By this time, Karel had joined an underground resistance movement against Joseph Stalin. I wasn't really interested in politics but Karel was and I soon came under his influence. Now, instead of reading Pushkin poetry and talking about Proust, we talked about Stalin and how terrible it would be if he should come to power.

In 1924, Lenin died and thereafter Stalin began his quest for power. There were many Russian Communist Party leaders who were in opposition to Stalin. The most important of the Oppositionists was Leon Trotsky. The Oppositionists wanted democracy within the Russian Communist Party. They were perfectly willing to have the Party run the country dictatorially but they wanted the Party itself to be run democratically. It meant that they wanted freedom of discussion about everything within the Party.

As Stalin's influence within the Russian Communist Party increased, the freedom to discuss various issues openly became more and more restricted. It became dangerous to express opinions if they did not coincide with the beliefs of Stalin or if they did not support the decisions made by Stalin. All public discussion of politics was stopped in the newspapers. Stalin said he stopped it because millions of Communists demanded it.

When the news of the government's censorship spread, many people found it hard to believe. They had believed, following the Bolshevik Revolution, that they would be allowed to express themselves about anything. It was then that Karel and his fellow underground workers secured a printing press by way of the black market. In Soviet Russia a person could get anything through the black market, "even Stalin's soul." Every week Karel and his comrades printed articles that explained the dangers of Stalin's actions.

In time, Karel and his comrades were able to get a copy of Lenin's last testament. In the testament, Lenin wrote that Stalin was very rude and not a loyal comrade. Of course, Lenin's testament was the most powerful piece of information that the underground movement had. They made thousands of copies of Lenin's last testament and distributed them everywhere and to as many people as possible.

Naturally, Karel and his comrades were afraid that the printing press would be found by the NKVD, so I solved this problem. I carried it with me in a box that was hidden in my two wheeled cart. The NKVD went wild and crazy. They searched everywhere for the printing press. They searched all the houses. One day, while they were going through our room tearing the floor apart and the walls, I rode into the yard of the NKVD building with the printing press. I tied my horse to the hitching post and there the printing press remained in the cart during the NKVD search.

In 1927 Karel and I moved to Moscow. Karel became more and more involved in underground resistance activities. I did not join the underground movement but one evening I was asked by the movement to deliver a message written on a slip of paper to the apartment of an Oppositionist. In the Soviet Union, at that time, several families would live in one apartment. For example, Karel and I lived in an apartment that had eleven rooms but eleven families inhabited the place. Each family was assigned one room and all eleven families shared one bathroom and one kitchen. Each family was also assigned a combination of short and long doorbell rings. Karel and I were assigned three short and five long rings.

The Oppositionist to whom I was sent had two short rings and one long ring. However, I made a mistake. I pushed two long rings and one short ring. When the apartment door that I rang opened, there appeared an NKVD man. In the corner of the hall, I saw a mannequin and I said very quietly "I would like to see the dressmaker." The NKVD man turned around and asked some

of the residents who had gathered in the hall if a dressmaker lived in the apartment. One of the females replied that there was a dressmaker. I was told to go
to the last door in the hall. After I knocked, I heard a woman say "Come in."
As I entered, I told her, loud enough so that the NKVD man could hear me,
that I would like to have a dress made.

"Who sent you?" she asked.

Without hesitation, I gave the name of a good friend who I had known at
the tea factory.

"Oh, yes," she said, as if she knew the person, and then she began to take
my measurements. Then she asked, "What material would you like?"

Since this dress would not be made anyway, I chose the most expensive
material. I then got very busy and designed for her my imaginary dress.

Meanwhile, I was contemplating on how to get rid of the message that I
was supposed to give to the Oppositionist. My impulse was to go to the com-
munal bathroom and flush it down the toilet. But I was concerned that this
would arouse the suspicions of the NKVD man. So, I asked the dressmaker
for a glass of water and I swallowed the secret message.

I asked her why the NKVD man was in the apartment. She replied that
there was living in the apartment a counterrevolutionary and the NKVD was
trying to catch the people who were his associates. Apparently, someone had
informed the NKVD that a person from the underground resistance movement was going to deliver a message to the counterrevolutionary. The NKVD
man was ordered to arrest every person who would push two short rings and
one long ring.

As I opened the door to leave, I said loudly "I think it will be a beautiful
dress." Almost immediately the NKVD man appeared and said, "I am sorry
comrade, you will have to stay here." I was detained in the corridor of the
apartment all night long while the NKVD man was waiting for the person
who was to deliver the secret message. Of course, that person was me but he
did not know that. Throughout the night, I thought of Karel and what he was
thinking since I did not return.

When I returned to our apartment the next day, I was told that the NKVD
had arrested Karel while he was attending an Opposition meeting. They had
taken him away.

But where was he? That was the question. Immediately, I left and went
to a nearby prison to inquire if a man who looked like Karel was being
detained there. No, I was told. There was no man in prison that fit my description of Karel. I went to another prison and then another. Karel was not in
these prisons.

During my search, I was told that there was an NKVD officer, some kind
of information officer, who had records on all prisoners and where they were
being detained. I went to his office and took my place at the end of a long line

of people. I stood in line for hours. When I finally spoke to the officer, he told me that he had no record of Karel.

I was advised to go to the largest prison in Moscow which was where political prisoners were kept. I went there but they did not give me a definite answer. They told me to return on the day of Karel's letter. Karel's letter was the first letter of his last name. Karel had four G-days in every month. On these days, I or any family relative was permitted to bring a package or some money to Karel. The money could be used to buy items from the prison store. Every prison in Moscow had a store.

On the first G-day, I returned to the largest prison in Moscow. I was told again that there was no man like Karel in the prison. Thereafter, I ran from prison to prison in search of my husband. I did this for three weeks on every G-day until I found him. He was wearing the same clothes and underwear that he wore at the time of his arrest. He had no toothpaste and no soap.

Before I was permitted to hand to the officials at the prison my package for Karel, I was required to fill out a form. Then I waited for a slip of paper stating that Karel had received the package. Karel was allowed to write on the slip of paper only his signature.

I brought a package to prison every week but I had no money to give to Karel. We had no personal possessions that I could sell except for Karel's books.

They were very rare books and it would have been relatively easy to sell them. But I decided not to sell them; they were Karel's books and they were important to him. So, to earn money I got a day job cleaning the city streets.

After Karel had been in prison for three months, I was notified that I should come to the prison. It meant that his case had been reviewed. I was told that he had been sentenced into exile. It was a sentence that I had expected; nevertheless, it was still devastating.

On the day that I said good-bye to Karel, I was brought to an empty room within the prison. There was only a table in the middle of the room and a chair on each end of the table. I took my seat at the table and waited for Karel's arrival. I did not have to wait long.

Karel was escorted into the room by an NKVD guard. I had promised myself not to be shocked but I was. Karel had always had an appearance of elegance. But he had not been allowed to shave. He had a beard and his hair had grown long. Yet, he was smiling.

The NKVD guard stood by the table and said, "You have fifteen minutes. You must not talk about life within the prison. You must not talk about anything political. You may only talk about family matters."

Before our visit, I had a million things that I wanted to say to Karel but now that we were together, I could not think of anything to say. I was sitting there trying to decide what my last words to Karel should be and how I should kiss him good-bye.

When the fifteen minutes were up, the NKVD guard told us to stop. He addressed me as Citizen. No longer would the authorities recognize me as a Comrade because I was married to a traitor [an "enemy of the people"]. "Citizen," he said, "you remain in your place." Then he said to Karel, "You get up." As Karel got up, I jumped up and before the guard could stop me Karel and I were in each other's arms. The guard pulled us apart swearing at us and he pushed Karel out of the room. When the door closed, I was alone and was convinced that I would never see my husband again.

I found out that the prisoners who were sentenced into exile would leave from a railroad station located in the city's suburbs. I and a large group of other women, about one hundred of us, went to the station where there was a long train waiting to transport the prisoners. About midnight, the Black Ravens arrived filled with prisoners. (see Glossary—Black Raven) They brought hundreds of prisoners who were to be escorted into the railroad cars. As the prisoners walked from the Black Ravens to the railroad cars, they began singing *The International*. They did this in protest to Stalin. These prisoners considered themselves the real revolutionaries, not Stalin and his Russian Communist Party. The crowd of women, many of them weeping, also began singing. Meanwhile, the NKVD guards began pushing the prisoners with their rifles. As they did, the women began singing louder and louder. It gives me goose bumps as I think back to that time.

I would not hear from my husband until his letter, addressed to me, arrived two months after his departure. He wrote that he was exiled to the town of Chita in Siberia. He was given a job working with a publishing house and he wanted me to come and join him. Shortly thereafter, I received another letter delivered by a man. From the second letter, I learned that Karel had started to organize an underground resistance movement in Chita.

I approached some of Karel's friends and asked them to get me a ticket to Chita. At that time, students attending institutions of higher education received from the government tickets to visit their families during the summer and winter vacations. Karel's friends in the underground resistance movement in Moscow were able to secure one of these tickets and they filled it out for me to travel to Chita. According to the ticket, my name was Nina Tarasova and I was a student at the Moscow Technical Institute.

The trip to Chita took five days but the train arrived late, some seventeen or eighteen hours late. Karel was not at the station to meet me but I learned later that he had come to the station many times. I had Karel's address and hired a horse and droshky to take me there. On the way, we passed Karel who saw me and yelled, "Nila" and then ran after us and jumped in the droshky.

In Chita, I assisted Karel and his comrades in the underground resistance movement. On one occasion, I was asked to deliver an important message to a famous Old Bolshevik who lived in exile quite a distance from Chita. Karel was not able to deliver the message because he was not permitted to leave Chita. He was required to report to the NKVD authorities every day.

The plan was to write the message inside of two Russian cigarettes which were to be carried in a cigarette case. There was a problem with this strategy. I did not know how to smoke and having cigarettes in my possession would look suspicious if I did not smoke. So, for two days, Karel and some of his friends taught me to smoke. I learned how to strike a match as if I had done it for years, how to light a cigarette and how to blow out the smoke.

The cigarettes within the case were arranged in a special way. There were six cigarettes in the right side and six cigarettes in the left side of the case when it was opened. The middle two cigarettes in one of the sides of the case were the cigarettes which held the secret message. I had to remember where the two important cigarettes were within the case. If anything went wrong, I was to swallow them.

I purchased a train ticket second class so that it would appear that I was a woman with means. While I was standing in the corridor of the railroad car looking out the window a very high NKVD official in the next compartment asked, "Will you give me a light?" He asked me my name and I told him Nina Tarasova.

He asked me to join him for dinner and I agreed. He ordered wine and we talked about many things. He told me that he was going to the same town where I was headed. He drank and the more he talked I realized that he had been ordered to arrest several Oppositionists. The Oppositionists were growing in number, he said, and the party of Stalin, he believed, needed to deal with them with greater severity. It was clear to me that the Old Bolshevik who I was to contact was among those the NKVD official was ordered to arrest. "You are exactly right," I said, "we must not show any softness. They must be stopped," I emphasized, "and if it's necessary to incarcerate all of them, then so be it."

Suddenly he said, "Oh my! What a shame! I'm out of cigarettes. Would you mind very much giving me one of yours?" His request caught me by surprise and my mind went blank. Were the cigarettes that I was to offer in the right side of the case or in the left side? Karel had shown me many times how to open the case so that a person would take a cigarette from the side that did not hold the secret message. However, my time to die had not yet come because the NKVD officer took a cigarette from the side of the case that did not hold the secret message.

We arrived at our destination the next day and I quickly left the train and made my way to the address Karel had given me. When I knocked, a woman in the house asked if I had a certain book. I was to say yes and I did. The woman told me that the Old Bolshevik was expecting me and she would take me to him that evening. I told her, "I'm afraid this evening will be too late." I explained that the Old Bolshevik might be arrested this evening. The woman understood and left to tell the Old Bolshevik to meet me at a specific location. If we felt that we were not being watched, I was to ask him for a match.

My rendezvous with the Old Bolshevik went well. When we met we talked as casual friends. I asked him if he wanted a cigarette and he said yes. By that time there were only two cigarettes left in the case, the two bearing the secret message. The Old Bolshevik took both cigarettes. I then returned to Chita without any incident.

I spent three weeks in Chita with Karel and they were like a honeymoon. Some friends gave us two pairs of skates and we spent the days skating, reading books and just being together. It was beautiful and peaceful and we were very, very, very happy. We had been married for three years but our time together in Chita made me realize just how wonderful life can be if one lives in peace and quiet with a husband. Karel and I decided that I should return to Moscow and make arrangements that would permit me to return to Chita to live with Karel in exile. So, I left Chita and returned to Moscow.

One evening, after I returned to Moscow, there was a loud knock on the door where I was staying. "Just a minute while I get dressed," I said. I was lying on the bed thinking about the simple weeks of friendship and love that Karel and I had spent together skating and walking in Chita. At the door there was an officer accompanied by two soldiers and the superintendent of the apartment building. The room was too small for all four to enter so only the officer came in leaving the door open so that the others could hear his conversation with me.

The officer was very young, he had blond hair, he was tall, he wore glasses, he looked intelligent, but he was cold and unpleasant.

"Citizen," he said, "this is an order for your arrest and an order to search your room." He then handed me the paper.

"I don't care to see it," I said.

"But, Citizen, under Soviet law you must read it and see that it is correct."

I smiled and said, "And if it isn't correct, what will you do?"

"In such a grave moment as this," he answered, "there is no time for a joke."

I took the paper. It was a form that had been filled out with my name and address. It did not say why I was being arrested except that I was being arrested for investigation and that my case was going to be studied.

"Now we will conduct a search," he said.

The officer searched everywhere with his cold protruding fish-like eyes until five o'clock in the morning. He then called one of the soldiers and ordered him to call for a car. He turned to me and said, "Citizen, get ready. You may take with you three changes of underwear."

"Don't worry," I told him. "I haven't three changes."

"You may take a toothbrush and soap," he said, "but no paper, no newspapers and no pamphlets of any kind."

In front of the apartment building there was parked a big, black, old fashioned car with large windows and high wheels. I said to the officer, "I know it will be a long time before I will see Moscow again. Do you mind if we go to the prison using the longer route?" He did not answer but we did take the longer route and we drove past Red Square, the Kremlin and the Moscow River. There was a stillness in the air as if nature had not yet awakened. Everything seemed so beautiful and I felt such sadness.

When we arrived at Lubyanka, the most horrifying prison, I was brought into a large bare room with two benches and a table. Shortly, a woman entered and told me to undress. I asked her what she wanted me to take off and she said, "Everything." She went through every seam with very quick experienced fingers while I stood naked watching her. Then she told me to lie down on one of the benches. I knew what she intended to do and told her "I want you to wash and dry your hands in my presence. Of course, you can refuse to do so and call soldiers who will hold me down, but I will fight. I am not a criminal," I said, "but a political prisoner." So, she called a soldier and he brought her a basin, a pitcher and a towel and she cleaned her hands. Then she searched me.

When I arrived at Lubyanka, I had my hair parted on one side with a comb. I was wearing shoes with laces and a cotton petticoat which was gathered with a string made out of the same material as my shoelaces. The woman examining me took the comb, the shoelaces and the string as a precaution to prevent me from hanging myself. I also had something pinned with a safety pin and she took that as well. "How do you expect me to wear my petticoat without that string?" I asked. "I don't know and I don't care," she replied. So, I got dressed wearing a short shift and my black tights that I wore whenever I went skating. That was all I wore. The woman left.

I sat alone in the examination room for a long time and became hungry. I got up and kicked the door. When a soldier came, I told him, "I'm hungry." He said, "Until all the procedures are finished, you will get no rations." "Make it quick then," I said. "Make it very quick."

At last a soldier brought me to a room with a window with metal bars and with a simple bed and one chair. He brought me black bread, vegetable soup, a hot liquid that looked like tea, and a little piece of sugar. The black bread was served on a metal plate and the bread was "magnificent." The tea-like drink was served in a metal container and I was given a metal spoon for the drink and the soup. I was surprised with the meal. This is not bad, I thought.

When I finished eating, the metal dishes were removed and I was left alone and locked up.

I sat for hours in silence. There was nothing to do. In time, I kept myself busy. I would imagine being in different places and talking to all kinds of different people.

In the evening, I was taken to a washroom which consisted of toilets and water basins. There were no showers. It was a male guard who brought me. There were no female guards except for the woman who had searched me. I was given five minutes to bathe. The walk to the washroom and the five-minute wash were welcoming activities. I was just twenty-two years old and I was a person who liked action. Seeing the water pouring into the basin was action and it pleased me. When the five minutes were up, the male guard knocked on the washroom door and announced, "The five minutes are up."

"I'm not ready." I said.

He knocked on the door again and said, "If you're not ready in two minutes, I'll come in." So, I got ready.

The guard took me back to the prison cell, brought me my supper and retrieved the metal dishes when I finished eating. Again, I was alone and locked up. I felt like a caged tiger. I walked forth and back, and forth and back and forth the length of the cell. I did pirouettes from the bed to the floor and from the floor to the bed. Every ten minutes, a guard came and looked through the little window in the door. When he saw me sailing through the air, he said that what I was doing was dangerous. He told me to sit down.

I decided to draw a mural on one of the walls within the cell. I took my tube of toothpaste and drew a picture of Stalin being taken to prison. My Stalin had a large mustache and was passing through the prison gates of Lubyanka. I had written the name Lubyanka over the top of the gates. The meaning of the picture was unmistakable.

When the prison guard saw the picture as he looked through the little window, he left to get the superior officer, the commandant. Seeing the picture, the commandant warned me that my behavior would result in greater punishment. He told the guard to wipe away the picture and take away my tube of toothpaste.

The next time that the guard looked through the small door window, he saw only a blanket with which I had completely covered myself. Meanwhile, I was rubbing my neck under the blanket. The guard thought I was trying to kill myself and he ran to get an officer. When the officer arrived, he ordered me to get up. I told him that I was not dressed. "Well," he said, "we will leave the room so you can dress." What I wanted was action. I wanted some kind of activity in which to participate.

The officer and the guard searched my cell for any instrument that I could use to commit suicide; they found nothing. "I must warn you," the officer said, "bad behavior will make more complicated your sentence. You must learn to be patient. Remember you are a prisoner." I retorted that I would never consider myself a prisoner (guilty of a criminal act).

I was a political prisoner and political prisoners were treated differently from criminals. You see, Stalin was not yet strong enough politically and so he proceeded against the members of the Opposition cautiously. The Oppositionists, at this time, were punished with light sentences. They were also given every opportunity to recant and support Stalin and his ideas. It was after Stalin banished Leon Trotsky from the Soviet Union, that he [Stalin] began to suppress the Opposition with greater stringency.

Seven days went by and nothing happened. Nothing happened. I began knocking on my cell door screaming, "I want to know the accusation. What have I been accused of?" The guard came and promised me that he would take my demand to his superior officer. Hours passed and nothing happened. Nothing happened. So, I took off my shoes and used them to hit the window in the cell, breaking the window. That brought the authorities to my cell. I finally got some action. They confiscated my shoes and put me in a cell in which the entire window was covered with a heavy netting. Thereafter, I was watched constantly.

I demanded a piece of paper and a pencil and wrote down that I had not yet been interrogated. I demanded that I be interrogated, that I be held in a cell with other people, that I be allowed to go for walks in the prison yard and that I be given reading materials. My complaints were forwarded but no answer was forthcoming.

Then one day a guard came and ordered me to get together my belongings. We walked a great distance to another cell which was occupied by seven women. I was familiar with two of the women. It was a comfortable cell. There were four bunks on one side and four bunks on the other side. Each bed had a big mattress and its own blanket. In the middle of the cell was a table. Some of the women had been detained in the cell for six months, some for four months and some for three months. I told them all what I knew. It was wonderful being with other human beings and each day passed quickly.

After three or four days, I was taken to Butirki Prison, an old prison dating back to tsarist days. It was divided into two parts—one part for political prisoners and one for criminals. I was taken to an empty cell, a narrow room with a small window. If I jumped up high enough, I could see beyond the bars that protected the window and into the prison yard. The narrow bed, the table and the chair were permanent fixtures attached to the wall. There was a pillow on the bed and a sheet made of course material.

A few days later, a nice young woman was brought into the cell. She was a Georgian and was terribly frightened. She was my age but I no longer felt like a young woman. [Nila was twenty-two years old.]

When I learned that she played the game of chess, we decided to make a set of chess pieces from the black bread we were given. The black bread was very chewy. We chewed it and shaped it into game pieces—kings, queens and horses. We made a beautiful chess set. We took a sheet of newspaper and on it we drew the chess board. Sometimes, we would play all night until the sun rose. Of course, she would always beat me but I was learning fast.

In the month of April, I joined the other political prisoners in a hunger strike. By this time, the authorities had removed me from my cell and they banished me to solitary confinement. I had angered them with my antics. They believed that my actions provoked the other prisoners and caused them to become unruly.

The hunger strike was started by a man whose pregnant wife was also in prison. The couple had two children and both were living outside of prison. Every day the wife went into hysterics and she would scream. My god, how she would scream! It was awful to hear.

The husband wrote a letter informing the NKVD that if his wife was not released immediately, he would go on a hunger strike. Under Soviet law, a prisoner was to be given a piece of paper and a pencil if he or she wanted to write a petition. When I learned about this I, along with others who were also in solitary confinement, decided to participate in the hunger strike. On the second of April, at seven o'clock in the morning, each of us, when we were given our breakfast, handed the guard a petition.

All the petitions listed four demands. First, we demanded that the pregnant woman be released and be allowed to reunite with her two children. Second, we demanded that political prisoners who were in solitary confinement be released and that in the future no political prisoners be punished with solitary confinement. Third, we demanded that the Oppositionists be given newspapers and magazines. Finally, we demanded that every prisoner be permitted to walk in the fresh air every day.

A little while later an important NKVD officer came to see me.

"Are you Shevko?" he asked.

"Yes."

"How old are you?"

"Twenty-two."

"I thought you were much older."

I did not reply.

He then said, "Your petition was received and it will be considered, but in the meantime I advise you most seriously to stop participating in the [hunger] strike. It will not lead to anything." He then left and for four days nobody came to the solitary confinement cells. Water was our only source of nourishment. It's a great way to lose weight.

Thereafter, the guard, every morning, opened my cell door to place in the cell my breakfast. I would tell him that I refused to eat it. He would reply, "It's not any of my business. I must leave it here." He would leave it there for twenty minutes while I would try not to smell the food. I would sit there in my cell and not look at the food.

Not eating was difficult during the first two days of the hunger strike but thereafter I began to experience a strange sensation; it was a feeling of lightness. I would look at objects and each object seemed to be making a distinct sound in my head. The table in the cell would sound like a symphony that had no melody.

On the fourth day of the hunger strike, an important officer told us that the hunger strike was a foolish endeavor. However, he announced that from then on every prisoner would be granted the opportunity to walk daily in the prison yard and no political prisoner, from then on, would be punished with solitary confinement. The concessions were welcomed but we told the officer that the hunger strike would continue until the pregnant woman was set free.

On the morning of the seventh day of the strike, an important officer announced that the NKVD had interrogated the pregnant woman and had decided to release her so she could be reunited with her two children. Apparently, news of our hunger strike had become known in Moscow and the authorities felt it was necessary to free the woman. Thus, the hunger strike came to an end.

In my cell I often thought of mother and hoped that she would not find out that I was in prison. But one day I received a *peredatcha* [a package] and as I looked at its contents, I knew that it had been sent by mother. The bread had been sliced and toasted in an oven so that it would keep for a long time. The bread was in a bag so that I could hang it up so that the rats would not get to the bread. The package also contained a piece of salted smoked ham, four hard-boiled eggs and some soap. Mother would send two more packages during my incarceration.

Many months later, I learned that a friend had written to mother informing her that I was in prison. Mother traveled to Moscow and went to the office of the NKVD. She got down on her knees before one of the officials begging him to permit her to see me. The official pushed her aside and ordered some of the NKVD soldiers to take her away.

It was still the month of April when I was taken from solitary confinement and dragged to another place of punishment within the prison, a place that was much worse. The incident that led to this development occurred while I was being led to the washroom. I broke away and ran down the hall lifting the slots on the outside of the cell doors. These slots could only be lifted from outside the cells so the guards could look in and see what the prisoners were doing. As I lifted the slots I yelled "Good Morning!" "Good Morning!"

When an officer saw me, he ordered the guard to stop me. The guard grabbed me but I screamed with all of my voice and all of my lungs. When other prisoners heard my screams, they assumed the guards were hurting me. So, they began beating on their doors, yelling and screaming. It took five guards to hold me. They dragged me over the cement floors to a punishment cell located in a tower that was called the Tower of Pugachev. [During the reign of Catherine the Great, Pugachev led a peasant rebellion and when he was finally captured he was brought to Moscow and detained in this tower. He was interrogated, tortured and executed.]

The stairs to the cell where I was to be held were designed like a corkscrew. The cell was dark and round in design but it had corners. Hanging from the walls were iron hooks and other instruments used to torture people. Of course, I thought this is it. This is where I will be tortured and killed. I went crazy. I screamed. I pounded on the door until I was completely exhausted and then I laid face down. I was terrified.

Throughout the rest of the day, I was left by myself in my new cell. Dinner time came and went. I beat the door and called out but nobody came. There was a stillness, a silence that one could almost feel. There was not a sound from inside the cell and none from outside. Supper time came and went but no food.

By this time, I needed to relieve myself. But there was no container within the cell, so I relieved myself in one of the corners. It was degrading. I felt like an animal but I had no choice. After I relieved myself, I took my underwear and covered my waste. Theodore Dostoyevsky once said that a human being's worst trait is that he or she is able to get used to absolutely anything. I believe that this is true. I know this from experience. The fact that I was forced to relieve myself like an animal was more hurtful than being dragged to the cell. It was worse than being left alone all day and night without food or water.

In the morning a guard brought me breakfast and some paper that I used to remove the human waste. I was allowed to wash myself and then I ate.

I was visited again on the second day of my stay in the cell of punishment but after that I was left alone for several days. I lay on the bed staring at the walls, at the instruments of torture hanging from the walls, at the narrow rectangular window in the cell door and at the locks on the door. The locks were old and each was almost as large as a notebook.

They punished me more than they had planned and I wrote a letter of protest. I wrote to the chief officer of the NKVD within the prison. I did not address the letter to the prison warden because I did not consider myself a prisoner. I had not committed a crime. In the letter, I demanded that I be supplied with books and newspapers and be allowed to walk in the prison yard. I also demanded companionship.

On the seventh day of my solitary confinement at around eleven o'clock in the morning I heard footsteps on the stairway to my cell. It was a guard. He entered the cell and told me to get ready for a walk. It was a nice surprise and it was a sunny day. The guard brought me to a small yard that was viewed by male criminals whose windows faced the yard. When the male criminals saw me, they exposed themselves to me. These men had been sitting in prison for years without a woman. I was shocked and horrified. I ran to the corner of the yard and stood there facing the wall.

The next time that the guard came to take me for a walk, I refused to go. The guard did provide me with books. I read what he brought me from the beginning to the end. I read the works of Victor Hugo, de Maupassant and Tolstoy and many more.

In time, I became very good friends with my guard. He was such a nice boy. His name was Peter. He was not good looking but he was attractive enough. He used to open my cell door and leave it ajar. Then he would sit on a bench just outside the door. I would sit in my cell and he would tell me about his life in the village where he grew up. Peter was a simple soldier who missed his village.

"Can you sing?" He asked me one night.

"Not very well," I answered.

"In the village we used to sing," he said, "but nobody sings in Moscow." So, I would sing this very old Russian song and the tears would well up in his eyes. The tears would gather in my eyes as well. Peter longed for his village and I missed Karel.

Peter never made love to me nor did any of the prison guards. If they had tried to take advantage of me, they would have been shot.

The tower consisted of seven cells and all the cells housed political prisoners, members of the Opposition. Some cells housed two or three men.

Incarcerated in one of the cells was an engineer. He was a young man and he was brilliant. He took a piece of iron from the bed in his cell and with it he was able to unlock his cell door. In the evenings, he would open his cell door and then unlock all the other cell doors in the tower. Each of us would leave our cells and sit on the steps of the spiral staircase and visit. We told the guards that if they reported us we would swear that they had opened our doors. We had an agreement with the guards, that should somebody enter the tower the guard at the bottom of the staircase would alert us by knocking on the railing of the staircase. We would then hurry into our cells and lock the doors. This happened just once. Virtually no one visited the tower.

We visited every evening from supper time till bedtime. We told stories, we told jokes, we sang and we recited poetry. The young engineer talked about engineering. A history professor who had taught at Moscow University gave us a whole series of lectures on Russian literature. In time, a certain bond or unity developed between us.

One day a guard entered my cell and said "Citizen, be ready with your things." I asked him where he was taking me but he did not say. After I gathered my things, he led me to the entrance gate of the prison. The gate stood open and I could see people in the street. One woman who saw me from afar made the sign of the cross at me. I wanted to meet her and speak with her but the guard hurried me on and led me to a cell in another building. Apparently, my confinement in the Tower of Pugachev was over. I had been confined in the tower for several months.

After supper, a soldier entered the cell to tell me to be ready with my things. I was brought to a large room within the office building of the prison. There must have been 200 to 250 women in the room. I recognized some of the women and we embraced and kissed and wept. My god, it was good to see them.

Shortly, an officer called out my name, "Citizen Shevko." I was told to step into another room where another officer sitting at a desk pronounced my sentence. "Nila Shevko, wife of a traitor to the Soviet state, is to be exiled for five years." I was not told why I was being exiled nor was I told where I was to be sent. I was, however, given a small piece of paper which bore my sentence. All the women were given a similar piece of paper; some were sentenced for three years, some for five years and some for six years.

About an hour later, some guards brought us outside into the fresh air. Waiting for us were five vehicles [Black Ravens]. They were parked as close to the door as possible. They were to take us to the railway station.

As we were transported to the station, I could see people walking the city streets. I was standing pressed against the small window of the rear of the van. I saw a boy kiss a girl in the doorway of a building. Some of the women in the van began to cry so I suggested that we sing *The Marseillaise.* (see Glossary—*The Marseillaise*) We must have sung loud enough for people in the streets to hear us because they stopped as we drove by and just stared at our vehicle [Black Raven]. I am sure that they told their families, later that day, that they had witnessed several Opposition women singing *The Marseillaise* as we were being hauled away.

At the railway station, we were marshaled into the cars of a very long train. Each car had been built the same. Each was furnished with hard benches and on every bench there was one blanket. There were bars at the windows and at each end of a car there was a guard.

It took us more than two weeks to arrive at our destination, which was the city of Sverdlovsk. Every morning we were each given a ration of bread, about two pounds for the entire day. They also gave us some kind of porridge, similar to oatmeal in texture and flavor and some hot soup.

At Sverdlovsk several vehicles [Black Ravens] were waiting to take me and about seventy other prisoners to our next destinations. We were removed from the train and the prisoners who remained on the train continued their journey to other destinations. Among those who were taken off the train were three women: me, an Old Bolshevik woman and another woman.

At the prison they took us into a large room that was empty except for two benches. Here we spent the night. The prison did not have cells for political prisoners, only cells for criminals, so in the morning the Old Bolshevik woman told an officer, "We want to be sure that women will not be put in cells with criminals." "All right," the officer said, "your demand will be satisfied." Given that assurance, the Old Bolshevik was led to a cell. She then wrote a note assuring me and the other woman that her cell held no criminals.

I was the last to be led to a cell. I was taken down a long, long corridor and from a distance I saw a person coming towards us. One of my guards told me to turn and face the wall. This was a policy in all the Soviet prisons. A prisoner was to face the wall whenever a person from the other direction approached. I turned to the wall slowly because I was very tired. But as I turned, I recognized the approaching prisoner, it was my husband. "Karel," I screamed. Before the guards were able to stop me, I ran to Karel and we put our arms around each other and hugged each other. I could feel my heart beating, it was sparked by my love for Karel. We didn't say a word. We just kissed and wept. It took all three guards, the two guards who were with me and the one with Karel, to pull us apart.

The guards took me to another building and into a narrow cell that housed sixty women. The cell was furnished with long benches against the walls, a long table and a smaller table in the center of the room. At the smaller table, there sat a beautiful woman with gold colored hair that she wore up in a swirl around her head like a crown. She looked at me with beautiful eyes and asked, "Political?" I reacted by saying, "Leave me alone." Then I explained what had just happened to me. The beautiful woman turned to another woman and ordered, "Get up and give her the [your] seat." The woman stood up immediately and I realized that the golden-haired one was the head of the cell. I took the woman's place, laid down, covered myself and rested there for two to three hours.

In the afternoon, the golden-haired one approached me and asked, "Can you work?" By this time, I had been informed who the golden-haired one was. She was Moura, a notorious bandit who was a famous bank robber. Her father was a Russian and her mother was a Gypsy. As a political prisoner, by law, I was not required to work. However, if I had refused to work, my life with Moura and the other women would have become difficult. I also wanted to keep busy. So, I answered, "Yes, of course I can work." Moura then ordered me to wash the floor. I turned up my sleeves and washed the entire floor. I did this every day, twice a day.

All the women in the cell were criminals. Among them were all kinds of thieves, prostitutes and murderers. I had with me paper and pencil and as a political prisoner I had the legal right to petition to be moved from the cell but I decided to stay. I preferred to remain with criminals. Living with political prisoners in a small cell room was strenuous. They argued constantly and they were always organizing some kind of movement. I was tired of it. I knew that if I was detained with the Old Bolshevik woman she would constantly be talking about the [Bolshevik] Revolution and how wonderful it was and what a pure Leninist she was. I enjoyed being with the criminals. They were interesting and time passed by quickly.

One day I saw the golden-haired Moura reading. "What are you reading?" I asked. "Karl Marx," she answered. Moura had some ten books. They were all political in content and authored by Communists such as Lenin and Stalin. Moura was an anarchist. She hated the Communist Party but she explained, "If you fight against somebody, you must know what they stand for."

There was an old lady among us who everybody called Grandmother. She was so clean and tidy. She wore white woolen stockings. She wore a black blouse with little pleats and she had white hair that she wore in a bun. She radiated cleanliness and there was a wonderful quietness about her. She was like an icon within the cell. (see Glossary—Icon)

Often the other women would ask Grandmother to tell them stories. She would tell them beautiful stories that had religious meanings about angels, God and Jesus Christ. She would tell the stories with a most even voice. She never repeated herself and the stories would go on and on. She would sit there with a group of listening women and she would look at them over the metal framed spectacles that she wore. Grandmother was so pure that dirt did not stick to her.

What was this old woman doing in prison incarcerated with criminals? No one ever talked about the crime that she had committed. So, one day I asked her why she was in prison. She replied, "I am here for life."

"But why?" I asked.

"Oh, my child! I killed my husband and my daughter."

"But why?"

"To save his [her husband's] soul."

Then she told me this story. One day while she was working in the field, she discovered her husband sleeping with their daughter. It was such a grievous sin. She took an ax and chopped off his head and then she chopped off her daughter's head. In order to save her husband's soul, she was serving a life term for murder. She had already spent many years in prison. Because of her good behavior in prison, she was offered parole but she rejected the offer. She wanted to die in prison. She wanted to suffer for her husband's sin and she believed that through her suffering she was paying for his sin and in turn saving his soul from damnation. At night, I would hear her pray with a whispered voice.

Because of the old woman and Moura, the golden-haired anarchist, our cell was orderly and everyone obeyed a code of morality. There was no lesbianism in our cell. In other cells lesbianism was a common practice and no one seemed opposed to it. Moura, however, made it very clear; there was to be no lovemaking in the cell. Anytime that she noticed two women lying together in a bunk, she would throw them out.

Of course, there were women who longed for some kind of sexual sensation. There was a woman in another cell with a baby. Whenever our cell door was open, she would come to the door with her baby. Some of the women in our cell would offer the mother money if she allowed her baby to suck their breasts. They would say, "I will give you five rubles if you let the baby suck at my breasts." The mother would then pass her baby from woman to woman to suck frantically at these dry things.

During my months in prison with the criminals, I would recite poetry and read literature. The criminals would sit on the benches and I would sit at one of the tables and for hours I would recite to them the poetry of Pushkin, Lermontov and Blok. Probably the poem that was most popular with the women was one that concerned a husband who discovered that his wife had been unfaithful. Upon his discovery, he locked her in her room and there she died. When the husband reentered the room, he found on the bed only his wife's skeletal remains and her hair. It was a tragedy and by the end of the poem a number of women were weeping.

I would also read to the women out of books that I requested from the prison library. One of the books was Tolstoy's War and Peace. I skipped the military descriptions because I did not think that they would hold the women's attention but I read the rest of the book. My inmates loved it; they did not even want to go for their daily walk. They preferred to listen to me read. I asked Moura if she wanted to read but she said "no." I assumed that she was not a strong reader and that she feared that if this became evident, it would jeopardize her authority within the cell.

We played cards, although it was against the prison rules to do so. Once a week, everybody was required to leave the cell and leave their personal items in the cell. The guards would then search for knives and for all other things identified as criminal. This included playing cards.

If they found any of these items, they would be confiscated. But by evening we were again playing cards. I do not know where they came from and I did not ask. They were put on the table and we played. We played mostly a game called twenty-one. We did not play poker. However, we did gamble, not for money, but for personal items such as shoes and clothes.

It was Moura who taught me how to tell a person's fortune by using playing cards. She believed strongly in the art of fortune-telling and showed me the procedure that she used. She would begin by asking a person "What do you want?" Then she would draw from the deck three cards and from the order and the meaning of the cards, she would give the answer. For example, if the three cards were sixes it would mean roads and that the person was going to travel. If all three cards were spades, it meant trouble. The ace of spades implied sickness, the ace of hearts predicted love and the ace of diamonds foretold the arrival of a letter. I became so adept at using the cards to tell a person's fortune that I was paid in money to do so. They called me the political fortune-teller or the counterrevolutionary fortune-teller.

My inmates would steal from each other. I had with me a beautiful necklace made in Constantinople. One day, I took it out and put it on and everybody admired it. Later, when I woke up from taking a nap, I discovered that the necklace was gone. It was upsetting and I announced out loud its disappearance. Moura responded by taking the lead. She approached each inmate by looking in their eyes and saying, "It must be back by midnight." Later, I would find the necklace under my pillow. Someone had placed it there after I went to sleep.

After a lengthy stay in Sverdlovsk, I was told that the authorities were preparing to transfer me out. I had become so involved with life in Cell Twenty-seven that the possibility of a transfer came as a shock. I was to learn about my new place of destination after I was called into the office of the commandant of the prison [the prison warden]. He told me that due to my bad behavior in Butirki Prison in Moscow, I was to be sent to Tabory, a place that was far to the north. It is near the Arctic Circle. It was said that if one left Tabory and traveled straight to the North Pole one would not come across anymore villages.

On the evening of the day when I was informed of my transfer, the guards came for me. I gathered my things and left. Grandmother crossed me with the sign of the cross many times and Moura gave me a good-bye kiss.

The transfer to Tabory began in a Black Raven which was used to take me from the prison to the railway station. From there, a train took me north to the last town on the railroad. There I joined 125 men who were also serving a sentence. It was winter and there was snow on the ground. So, we were each given a *polushubok* which is a knee length coat made of sheepskin, a hat made of artificial fur and heavy boots. I was grateful to God that I had such large feet. The boots were big but not too big. All of these items were given to us free of charge; we were also promised thirty rubles a month. We were organized in a long row and we began our long walk which would take several weeks.

On the first day of our long walk, we did not go far because no one was accustomed to walking long distances. But thereafter, we walked between fifteen and twenty kilometers [9 to 12 miles] a day. I did not mind it at all. After sitting for months in a prison cell, I was now walking in the cold fresh air surrounded by beautiful nature. My god, I enjoyed it! We walked only during the day and we would stop when we arrived at a large barrack surrounded by wire. Here we would spend the night.

Along the way, our number became smaller and smaller as prisoners were assigned to the different villages through which we walked. In time, there were only five of us left on the long walk. It was very cold but it didn't feel cold. The snow was dry and beautiful. Everything was beautiful, the huge pine trees and the evergreens. The sky was clear and blue and there was present a wonderful quietness. The beauty of the environment erased from my mind the dirty prisons in which I had been confined, the dirty faces of the inmates, the smell of filth and the dirty stories.

Whenever we arrived at a village where we were to spend the night, the guard would assign us to families that would feed us and provide us with a place to sleep. The peasants gave us big bowls of soup, huge pieces of meat, cottage cheese made from whole milk and big bowls of sour cream. We were given homemade bread and dried fish. All of it was delicious. The diet of the people in northern Siberia was superior to the diet of the citizens in Moscow.

After many weeks of walking, we arrived in Tabory in the early afternoon. The village consisted of twenty-four houses, a post office and an NKVD office which was the place of residence for the local NKVD officer. The officer had been banished to Tabory as punishment for some kind of misdemeanor. Nevertheless, he was still an NKVD officer.

When we entered the NKVD office, the officer was sitting in his underwear, his feet were soaking in hot water, he was perspiring and he was drinking from a bottle of vodka. He was the most unrepresentative authority I had ever seen. Our guard gave him the envelopes with our names and sentences. The officer informed us that we were permitted to walk about the village freely but he warned us that if we left the village and were caught beyond a two kilometer distance from the village, we would "be punished." We were required every evening to report to the NKVD officer.

The first time that I walked the street that ran through the village was a sensational experience. I walked up and down the street tasting freedom, with no guard beside me. A young boy ran up to me and asked, "Are you one of us?"

"And who are you?" I asked.

"I am one of the Oppositionists."

The boy took me to a house and in time all the Oppositionists in the village came to the house to welcome me. They brought vodka and prepared a meal. We drank vodka and made several toasts such as "Down with Stalin!"

Altogether, there were some sixty people living in exile in Tabory. Including myself, there were nineteen Oppositionists. There was a large group of Zionists and some anarchists and Mensheviks.

There were only three female Oppositionists but when one of the women became ill, she was sent away. So, it was just me and another woman and we shared a tiny room that the NKVD had taken from a peasant family.

The woman I roomed with was as dry as hay. She would never visit. She only preached communism. From the time she woke up early in the morning, she would quote Lenin. "On page such and such, Lenin said. . . . " I could care less what Lenin said. This woman did not care about clothes or anything else, except Lenin.

After a while, I asked the NKVD officer to let me work with the village peasants. There was plenty of work to be done and I needed the money. I was receiving from the State just six rubles a month and that was very little. The NKVD officer agreed to let me work and the work varied. For example, I learned to spin raw wool into thread, which was done in the winter. My favorite job was going into the nearby forest to chop wood. I was accompanied by a village peasant girl. We would walk to the forest but before we began working, we would lie down in the snow and look at the trees all covered with snow and shining like millions of diamonds. It was wonderful being close to nature and it was so quiet. The wood we chopped was stacked in piles and when the sleds arrived, we would load the sleds with the wood. At noon, a man would arrive who prepared our dinner over an open fire. The smell of the food and the freshly cut wood, I still remember. It is a wonderful memory.

The men in the village hunted the wild game which was in abundance. A man might come home with two or three bears that he had killed. The skins of the bears would be used as covers for the sleighs. From the more tender meat, the women would make *pelmeni*, which was prepared in the following manner:

The tender meat was cut into small pieces. Chopped onions and peppers were added to the meat. Small portions of the mixture were then rolled in a thin square sheet of dough. They were then placed on large wooden trays and brought outside. After they were frozen, they were put in bags that were sewn for this purpose and the bags were hung in a small building located near the family house. A bag of *pelmeni* would feed several people after the *pelmeni* was boiled in water. A sauce made with pepper and mustard would be poured over the *pelmeni* to give it extra flavor.

The men in the village also hunted for wild birds. They would take an empty wagon in the summer and three days later they would return with the wagon full of birds. The wild ducks were delicious. The meat was so tender; it could be cut with a fork.

The nearby river had an abundance of fish. Catching the fish was easy. All one had to do was take a metal hook and attach to it a piece of cloth. One did not have to wait long to catch a fish.

One of the great pleasures in Tabory was the arrival of mail. There was no telephone and no telegraph in the village. The mail arrived once a week on Wednesday. On that day, the exiles strained to hear the ringing of bells. The mail was delivered in a sleigh pulled by three horses and the middle horse was decorated with bells. On a winter day, a person could hear the approach of the mail from miles away. It was then that one could hear people yell, "The mail is coming!" This would be followed by people running to the post office. Of course, the exiles did not know what to expect. It could be good news or bad news. One might receive a letter, books, a parcel or some other item. To this day, whenever I hear the ringing of bells, I think of Tabory by the Arctic Circle.

I had always wanted to learn a foreign language, so I asked one of the Jewish exiles to teach me the Hebrew language. His name was Ashkinazi and he was well known. He agreed to teach me and every day he would teach me to converse and write. The writing was done from right to left which was fascinating. It did not take long before I began to speak with a heavy accent and use gestures.

It was at Tabory that I was introduced to collectivization. Stalin had decided to organize all of Russia's agricultural land into collective farms. The NKVD officer in the village received orders that he was to register all the native villagers. The officer called a meeting but the exiles were not invited because we were prisoners. However, the village family with whom I lived told me about the meeting. It was apparent that they did not fully understand collectivization.

After I had been in Tabory for a year and a half, the prisoners in the village decided that it was necessary to purchase supplies from another village. Our alcoholic NKVD officer gave us permission to send two prisoners with a horse and wagon to a village fifteen to twenty miles away [24 to 32 kilometers away]. An elderly gentleman who had been a professor and I were assigned to carry out the expedition. We were told by the NKVD officer that we had to be back within thirty-six hours.

The professor and I discovered that the prices for the items we had come to purchase in the nearby village were reasonable. Assuming that they would be even lower in the next village, we traveled to that village and we were right. With the money that we had received from our fellow exiles, we bought a pig, a big fat one. We purchased long salted fat strips and many pig legs. We bought lots of onions on strings and potatoes and garlic. We piled the wagon high. I also practiced my fortune-telling skills in exchange for eggs, ham and sausages. However, we lost track of time and when we got back to Tabory we had been gone for seventy-two hours.

We reported back to the NKVD officer and explained to him why we were delayed. We had gotten caught in a violent storm, which was true. One of the wheels on the wagon broke and needed to be repaired and we encountered other time-consuming problems. He told us that he had already sent out a report that two of his exiles had escaped.

In time some NKVD men arrived in Tabory to question the professor and me about our absence from the village. We told them about the storm and the other problems which delayed our return. The NKVD men decided that the professor should remain in Tabory but I should be transferred to another location.

That evening, my village family gave me a farewell dinner in the kitchen where we ate all our meals. We drank some vodka and we talked. They asked me why I was being taken away and the women wept, no they wailed. In Russia at a funeral the louder the people cry, the more they express their love for the deceased. That is what the women in my village family were doing.

The NKVD men and I traveled in a droshky pulled by three horses with bells. [A droshky is a low, four-wheeled open carriage pulled by horses.] I remember lying in the back and watching the road speed by. How I longed to settle down somewhere! I no longer had a desire to travel. I did not know what lay ahead. The future was unknown and uncertain. For me, the sounds that the bells were making were sad as they accompanied my sad thoughts.

We traveled by droshky for maybe a week. We would come to a place and change horses and then we would travel on. In the evenings we would stop at a peasant's house and eat and sleep. The trip by droshky came to an end when I was placed on a train which would bring me to Sverdlovsk. In Sverdlovsk, I was detained for two or three weeks in a prison cell.

From Sverdlovsk I was sent by train to Tyumen, in central Siberia. I was put in a compartment with two guards. All day long and day after day we would play cards. When we arrived at a station, we would put the cards away in case an officer should come by. Then, as the train left the station, we would get back to playing cards.

The cards were old, dating back to tsarist days. They were heavy and greasy to the touch. They were precious things. I still remember that one of the corners of the king of diamonds was missing. We played for money and with my Gypsy touch, I usually won.

At one of the larger railroad stations, I saw a family of peasants. Their little boy was wearing bast shoes, called *lapti*, and his little coat was made of homemade material. He walked up to me and gave me a coin, a kopek. The gift was interesting for in old Russia people believed that if you gave a kopek to a prisoner, then something very good would happen to you. I said to the boy, "I hope that you will be lucky." I kept the kopek for quite a long time. I hoped that something good would happen to me as well. [The kopek was the smallest Russian currency. The Russian ruble was divided into 100 kopeks.]

When we arrived in Tyumen, I was taken to the NKVD office and detained in one of the rooms. Eventually, I was taken into an office used by a big, good looking and important NKVD officer. He stood up and very politely asked me to sit down. It was the first time any NKVD man ever asked me to sit down and I assumed that I was to be shot. Politeness comes before death. I was struck by fear and perspiration gathered on my temples.

I remember sitting on the edge of the chair in front of the desk and the officer sat behind the desk holding a pencil with a happy expression on his face.

"Would you like a cigarette?" he asked.

"I don't smoke," I answered.

He put a cigarette gracefully in his mouth and lighted with a match.

"Nila Ivanovna, I am sure that you have heard that the most important Oppositionists have decided that their opposition is very dangerous for Russia. They have already come to Moscow. Would you like to join them? All you must do is write down that you agree to join them and sign your name to the letter."

I told him, "I have to think about it."

"How long will it take you?" he asked.

I told him that I did not know. I said that this was an important decision and one that I could not make alone.

"Don't you know that your husband has already signed and that he is on his way to Moscow?"

"No, I didn't know," I answered. "Am I free to go about town?"

"You are absolutely free," he said, "and I will give you the names of the Oppositionists in town and you can go and ask them [talk to them]."

The conversation was civil and elegant. What if this NKVD officer offered me his hand to say good-bye. Should I shake the hand of the NKVD which has imprisoned me and treated me so badly?

Happily, he did not offer me his hand; he just brought me into another office where a man gave me the names and addresses of three or four members of the Opposition. One of them was a woman with whom I was familiar and I went to see her. She said that she had not signed the letter; she was waiting for the decision from Moscow. She said a large boat was arriving from Tobolsk and it was carrying important Oppositionists who had signed the letter. A famous large prison was located in Tobolsk. Following the Bolshevik Revolution, this prison was used to detain many nobility and high ranking clergymen. Now it was used to imprison important Oppositionists.

We hurried to the place where the boat had just arrived. We saw many men on board. They were waving and shouting and seemed very happy. The gang plank was lowered and suddenly I saw Karel walking down the plank. He was wearing an old green soldier's coat with a rucksack on his back. His hair was quite gray. I was shocked and speechless. He walked past me just a few feet away. I cried out and he turned around and ran back and within seconds we were embracing each other. Together, we returned to the woman's apartment.

Karel told me he was very disappointed with the Opposition. He realized that should the Opposition come to power, there would be a change of words but no real change. There would be no freedom of expression. He said that he had suffered more than enough for the Opposition which he considered a lost cause. Karel told me that he had been held in a death cell for eight and a half months without a trial. Finally, he was given a ten-year prison sentence and was then transferred under guard to Tobolsk where, for many months, he was held in solitary confinement.

Karel was supposed to go on to Moscow that very night but he went to the NKVD and requested that they postpone his going for three days. They agreed to do so and in a polite manner. The woman [who was also an Oppositionist] wanted to give us some privacy so she moved temporarily and gave us her room.

I signed the letter while Karel was with me and sent it to Moscow. I then had to wait for its return from Moscow which took another three weeks. When it arrived, I left. For the first time in many long months, I felt free with no restrictions. Feeling that way, I went on to Moscow to rejoin Karel who had left for Moscow earlier.

We had no apartment in Moscow but Karel had a friend. He was an important Communist who had a country place in a Moscow suburb called Silverwoods. This friend permitted Karel to use the place. He himself was living in an apartment in Moscow. So, this is where we stayed but only for a short while. I didn't like the place. It was large and pretentious. I did not belong there. Karel understood. So, I packed up my belongings, got on a bus and headed for Moscow. Rather quickly, I found a room and shortly thereafter Karel joined me.

Karel was given a job in a publishing house and I found a job with the Moscow Association of Co-operatives. I worked for the association for five years and I was very happy and content.

Then suddenly Stalin initiated what became known as the Great Purge [Great Terror]. In December 1934 [Sergei] Kirov, one of Stalin's important lieutenants, was assassinated. It was rumored that Kirov was killed by a young man because he [Kirov] was having an affair with the young man's wife. Stalin, however, used the murder of Kirov as an excuse to liquidate the

Opposition. What followed was the Great Purge. Most everybody who had ever opposed Stalin was arrested.

Karel and I were visiting my mother when it was reported that many arrests were being made. Karel knew what that meant. "That is the end for us," he predicted.

We returned to Moscow and discovered that our room had already been searched. Our landlady was in complete hysterics. The NKVD men who had searched our room had not asked for me but they had asked for Karel. Most of the Opposition who had returned from exile had rejoined the [Russian] Communist Party but Karel had not. This, we felt, could be used against Karel.

A week passed and nobody came to arrest us. Then another week came and passed. Meanwhile, Karel was told at the publishing house that he was no longer employed there. A week later, I lost my job without any explanation. I was ordered to write down that I wanted to be relieved of my work. Karel tried to find employment but no one would hire him. A fourth week passed and no one came. Every evening we expected to hear a knock on the door and see a Black Raven waiting to take us away. The waiting drove us both crazy with anxiety.

Finally, Karel decided to call the NKVD to tell them that if they were not going to arrest him, he would leave and go somewhere else to find a job. The man Karel talked to on the telephone said he would like to see Karel and that he could meet with him at eleven o'clock or at three o'clock.

"Must I bring my things with me?" Karel asked.

"Not necessary," he replied.

"I will be there at three o'clock," Karel said.

To pass the time, Karel and I went to the theater to watch a French picture, "*Sous les Toits de Paris*." Following the movie, we walked to the NKVD headquarters. Karel first entered a small building to get his pass and then we walked to a door where Karel hesitated for a moment. He took off his hat, put his hand to his mouth and went inside.

I went right home because in Moscow a citizen was not permitted to stand near the NKVD building for any length of time. That evening, I waited for Karel's return. I waited and waited. Eight o'clock, nine o'clock, ten o'clock, eleven o'clock and twelve o'clock came and went but Karel did not return. I decided that Karel had been arrested. When Karel's letter-day came, I went to the prison to deliver a package. It was accepted.

Those who were arrested were accused of having a part in the murder of Comrade Kirov. Fear spread and friends were not able to help. I was afraid to walk the streets for fear that I might meet friends. I knew that it would be embarrassing for them not to greet me and speak to me; if they did, they might be arrested as well. The fear was so great that people did not go places.

There was a noticeable silence in Moscow; it seemed to hang over the city like a heavy cloud.

I finally got a job working in a large grocery store. A man who lived in the house where I lived, got me the job. I worked in the basement of the store sorting apples, the rotten ones from the good ones. I would take bites from some of the apples that were thrown away. The apples were a part of my diet along with black bread and scraps. Meanwhile, I tried to bring to prison all that Karel needed.

One day, I received a little card telling me to bring to prison Karel's clothes. I brought his coat but the prison authorities would not permit me to see Karel. I was told that Karel was to be transferred to Kolyma where they were mining for gold and where they were building a road.

In time, I received one postcard that Karel sent me while he was being transferred and two letters after he arrived in Kolyma. That is all I received from Karel. Then, for eight months, I did not hear from Karel or about Karel. [Nila had become the wife of an "enemy of the people."]

I finally heard about Karel's death one day while I was walking down the street. A man walking behind me said very quietly, "Don't turn around. Just keep on walking and listen to what I am about to say. I was in Kolyma and I saw your husband working there. It was very cold and he was wearing this thin, ragged coat and he eventually got pneumonia and died. I myself saw him dead." Later, I received from the NKVD a letter informing me that Karel had died from natural causes.

The State now recognized me as a widow of a prisoner [an "enemy of the people"], not as the wife of one. That made a huge difference and with that new identification I was able to get a job working for a newspaper, the *Journal de Moscou*. The newspaper had about 75,000 subscribers and of that number only about 1,000 copies were distributed in Moscow. All the other subscribers lived in France and other countries. Everything in *Journal de Moscou* was published to reflect the good life in the Soviet Union. Everything that was invented, that was painted and that was composed in the Soviet Union was reported for the readers abroad. Editorials and important articles, of course, had to be submitted to the Foreign Office for the approval of Maxim Litvinov, who was then the Foreign Commissar. All articles had to pass by the censor.

Everyone who worked on the newspaper was required to attend the meetings conducted by an organized political circle. In the Soviet Union there was a political circle in every plant, factory office, school and university which had as many as five people on its rolls. The instructors within a political circle were chosen by the local Communist Party and they were to indoctrinate the workers of plants, or factories or institutions in Marxism—Leninism. In this way the State gained control over the minds of the workers.

Among the translators who worked for the *Journal de Moscou* there was a Russian count, Count Vladimir Golitzin. He was very thin and was poorly dressed, yet there was a certain elegance about him. It was in his blood; he had received it through the milk of his mother. He was a Russian noble, a count.

He was quiet and rarely talked. Though he was nobility, the Communists did not arrest him because he could speak and write the French language with excellence and the authorities wanted the paper to look like it was originally written in the French language. Count Vladimir faithfully attended the meetings held by our political circle but I always felt that he was present in body but absent in spirit.

One day, the instructor who presided over our political circle suggested as a subject for discussion the following: What will life be like for people who live in a society that is totally socialist? [At every meeting there was a subject for discussion.] The instructor then asked each person in attendance to comment on the subject. Almost everyone's comments reflected what they had read in Stalin's writings. They tried hard not to express their own opinions or convictions. Towards the end of the discussion, on this particular day, the instructor turned to Count Vladimir and asked, "What do you think, Comrade Golitzin?"

"What do I think?" he replied. He took a long deep breath. He folded his hands together beneath his chin as if in prayer and with eyes closed, he said, "When socialism is built, there will be in every house, in every apartment, on every corner of the street, a faucet, and from this faucet will flow a wonderful dry champagne." Then he scratched lightly his chin and added, "Not sweet, but very dry. Somewhat like Cliquot."

We were completely spellbound as we imagined all the faucets and the aroma of champagne. The Count expressed himself so vividly that we could almost taste the champagne. The instructor pulled himself together and said, "Comrade Golitzin, what a strange idea of socialism." The Count just shrugged and that was the last time that I would hear him speak.

I worked as a reporter for the paper and one of my most successful interviews was with Mikhail Nesterov. He was a Russian painter who became famous during pre-revolutionary times. He refused to recognize the Soviet Union. But because he was such a great artist, Lenin ordered that no harm should come to him. He was given the highest food rations and the paints that he needed were delivered to him on a regular basis.

For twenty years Nesterov lived in a house just as he did before the Bolshevik Revolution. It was a lovely house with a beautiful garden. It was a piece of old Russia right in the heart of Moscow.

The managing editor of the paper, *Journal de Moscou*, learned that Nesterov was working on a portrait of Academician Ivan Pavlov, who was very distinguished because of his theory of condition reflexes. He called me into his office and told me that it would be great if I wrote a story about the portrait painted by Nesterov and to also get a photograph of the painting. It would be a challenge but I love challenges.

So, I put on my good gray suit and when I say good, I mean good. By this time, I was making more money than the editor. I was never on salary; I was paid entirely by the value of the article that I submitted. If it was an important story, I would receive about 125 rubles and if it was not so important, I received fifteen or twenty rubles. I wrote about everything: exhibitions, sports, fashions, movies and theater productions. In one edition I had seven stories.

On my way to Nesterov's house, I bought a bunch of violets. They were in full bloom at that time. When I rang the doorbell, a woman dressed as women dressed one hundred years ago came to the door.

"I brought some flowers for Mr. Nesterov," I said.

The woman looked surprised. "Will you wait outside?" she said.

"No," I said, "I will wait inside."

She went away and in a moment or two I heard her open a door and say "There are some flowers for you."

When Mr. Nesterov appeared, I quickly approached him with the flowers. "I want you to have these flower," I said.

"Why?" he asked.

"Because I need your help and because I love your work. I know that you have finished a portrait of Pavlov and I very much want to see it. I have just recently started reporting for the *Journal de Moscou* and I am sure the French people would love to hear about your work and see this latest picture."

"But I give no interviews to the Soviet papers," he said.

"It's not for the Soviet [Union]," I explained. "I want the world outside to see your painting."

He said that he would think about it but in the meantime if I would like to look at the painting, I could. I entered the room and there it was, a huge painting. It was covered but he uncovered it and as he did, I saw a most powerful portrait. It was magnificent.

Then we talked and I suggested that we write the article together. "I'm afraid," I said, "my knowledge is not sufficient to write it as it ought to be written and, besides, it will be much more important if you lend your name to it."

He was charmed by my proposition and we wrote a beautiful story, which Nesterov practically dictated. Thereafter, a photographer, who I had brought with me but who was waiting outside in the street, was brought in to take photographs of the painting. Many photographs were taken and the article was a huge success.

Though I was earning a good income, I was faced with a serious problem. It happened when the woman with whom I lived, since I returned from exile, told me to leave. She said, "I don't want to have the widow of a counter revolutionist living in my house."

There was a law in the Soviet Union which stated that a landlady was not permitted to force a resident to leave. She was allowed to ask a resident nicely and the two might come to a friendly agreement; but the resident did not have to leave unless a court of law required the resident to leave. Thus, I was summoned to court and my unpleasant landlady behaved in a mean and base manner. She shouted that having a widow of a counter revolutionist was a disgrace, she being a staunch Soviet citizen. The court must have agreed because I was given three months to find another place of residence.

I had to find another place to live. A friend told me that she knew of a woman who lived in a one room apartment that was divided in half by a partition that did not reach the ceiling. She and two of her children lived in one half of the room and her older daughter lived in the other half. I approached the woman and she offered to let me live with her older daughter for 200 rubles a month.

I was pleased with the offer but I was not sure that the militia would allow me to live there. In the Soviet Union when a citizen moved into another apartment, she or he had to present her or his passport [internal passport] to the local militia. The militia would examine the passport and would either assign or not assign the person to the requested place of residence. In the Soviet Union every citizen when she or he reaches the age of eighteen must appear before the local militia and apply for a passport and thereafter must reappear before the militia for an annual check-up. Written on the passport was a citizen's place of residence and the citizen was not to move to another place without the militia's approval. If a citizen decided to go on a vacation, she or he must first go to the militia to seek permission to stay, for a period of time, at the vacation spot. To lose one's passport in Stalin's Soviet Union was a huge tragedy.

I decided to take my passport to a top official in the local militia. I further decided to play on two human weaknesses, greed and vanity. So, I took with me 3,000 rubles and a Leica camera, which I borrowed from one of the newspaper's photographers.

At the militia headquarters, I was brought into the office of a top official. He was dressed in a typical military uniform. For several quick seconds, I studied the official trying to decide which of my weapons I should use. When I saw his eyes soften at the sight of the camera which was hanging in front of me from my neck, I judged that vanity should be my weapon.

I told him, "Comrade Chief, I am a reporter and our paper wants a story about and a photograph of one of the best militia chiefs in Moscow." The weapon was perfect; he was already posing at the table.

I asked him some questions and then I took photographs from every angle, though I had never taken a photograph before. I learned later that there was no film in the camera. I took photographs of him full-faced and sideways. Then I stood on a chair and took a photograph of him from above. "Now holding a pencil please," I said. He was very impressed.

After I shook his hand and headed for the door, I turned casually and said, "By the way, I forgot to ask about a little favor [that] you can do for me. I'm moving into a new apartment and must have permission [to do so]."

Without looking at my name or where I lived, he rang for an assistant and said, "Please see that this passport is taken care of personally." In five minutes, I had a fresh stamp with a signature on my passport, [internal passport].

So, I moved and I was very happy with my new residence. The children loved me, especially the older daughter who was seventeen years old. I read to her and discussed many things with her for by this time I had already experienced a full life. Her mother and I also got along very well. I told her about Karel and she accepted the facts like a true peasant woman. She was not afraid to be living with the widow of a counter revolutionist [an "enemy of the people"]; she sympathized with me and was sorry for my loss. She treated me like family.

Our room was part of an apartment that before the [Bolshevik] Revolution had belonged to a wealthy family. It consisted of eleven rooms, one kitchen and a toilet. In old Russia, the toilet was separate from the bathroom. The apartment originally had a bathroom but for the past three years an old woman with her cat was living in the bathroom. The bathtub had been cov ered with a piece of board and that was the old woman's bed.

I was told that soon after the old woman moved into the bathroom, the other occupants of the apartment had a meeting and decided that the old woman must be moved out of the bathroom so that they could use the cold water and tub to wash their clothes. The old woman refused to vacate the bathroom. The occupants then drafted a petition pointing out that they needed the use of the bathroom. The petition was sent to some lower authorities and they agreed that the old woman should move from the bathroom.

The old woman then brought her appeal to some higher authorities and they referred the case back to the lower authorities and ordered them to examine the case again.

One evening, while I was sitting in my room, the old woman scratched on the door of the room that I shared with the older daughter. I asked her to come in. She was wearing rubbers but no shoes. The rubbers were tied with a rope and her body was covered with a handful of rags. She had heard, she said, that I worked on a newspaper and she wanted me to write about her case. I couldn't do that. Her case could not be the subject of an article in a propaganda paper that was designed to appeal to people who lived abroad. However, I was able to give her, now and then, some pieces of bread and some soup which I am sure she shared with her cat.

Altogether, there lived in the apartment at the least thirty-two people. Each of the eleven rooms was occupied by a different family of three or four or five. On the door of the toilet there was posted a list of people who were required to keep the toilet clean. If in one room there were housed four people, then the occupants of that room were required to wash the toilet twice as often as the people that lived in a room with only two occupants.

At first, my landlady and I took turns cleaning the toilet. Later, I paid her to take my turn. Still later, I began using a public toilet because it was much cleaner than ours. We lived in Arabat Square. Our window faced the square and every morning I walked across the square and used the public toilet there.

When the entire apartment belonged to just one family prior to the Bolshevik Revolution, they had a large cooking stove in which they burned wood. That stove was now used by two families and all the other families used small kerosene stoves. The kitchen walls were lined with small tables and on top of the tables were these kerosene stoves. Because kerosene was rationed and very expensive, everybody accused everybody else of stealing their kerosene. I witnessed a woman lock the lid to her cooking pot to prevent the other occupants from stealing her food.

One of the most important events in my life occurred at a skating rink in Moscow in November of 1936. I loved to skate and I was very good at it. One evening, while I was skating, I saw in front of me a figure who was unsure on his skates and who eventually fell. I helped the person to his feet and noticed, by the way that he was dressed, that he was a foreigner. He thanked me in Russian with a bit of an accent and I went on my way. In Russia it is considered impolite for a woman to talk to a man to whom she has not been introduced, especially if he is a foreigner. However, as I continued skating, I kept my eyes on him and I noticed that he kept his eyes on me.

He fell again and again I assisted him to his feet. "It looks like I will have to help you," I said.

"Will you?" he asked.

"I can even teach you to dance," I told him. I took his hands and proceeded to lead him through different steps as the orchestra played the *Blue Danube Waltz*. Very soon we found that we could move rhythmically together. We never spoke a word; we were concentrating on our dance. The evening was perfect. It was all so perfect, the music, the cold sharp air, the lights and the people skating so gracefully. I suppose it was the beginning of a love affair.

When the orchestra stopped playing, we talked. He told me that he was an American and had come to the Soviet Union for one year to gather material on Russian folklore, both old and new. I told him that I worked on the *Journal de Moscou*. Eventually, one of his friends at the skating rink called out to him in English, "Robert, come here!" I will never forget the call. Robert excused himself and I left.

Several days later, I was more formally introduced to Mr. Robert Magidoff at my desk. Robert asked me for a walk and, without any hesitation, I agreed. It was a decision which could have led to serious consequences. By this time, hundreds of Soviet citizens, due to their connections with foreigners, had already been arrested. Yet I was in love and so was Robert. He suggested that we get married. I gave his proposal a lot of consideration and decided against it. Robert's stay in the Soviet Union was almost over and I was sure that the authorities would not permit me to leave the Soviet Union. Being separated from each other would be difficult for us both, especially if I became pregnant.

A wave of new arrests began in 1937. Most of the victims were the wives of men who had been arrested and declared guilty of being counter revolutionists; these were men who had opposed the rise of Stalin ["enemies of the people"]. A strong uneasy feeling entered my being. Karel had been identified as a counter revolutionist. More than a year had passed since his death but I felt sure that his fight against Stalin had not been forgotten. How right I was.

One day, on my return home, my landlady, in Russian fashion, greeted me with her hands clasped in front of her and her body swaying from side to side. A militia man had been at the apartment with a summons. I was required to appear on a certain date at the regional headquarters. I knew what that meant. The militia had initiated a new policy. Instead of arresting people at their places of residence, they summoned their victims to the militia headquarters and from there they were sent to their places of exile.

I telephoned Robert and told him that we must see each other at once. When we met, he could tell by the expression on my face that what we had feared would happen, did happen. He immediately begged me to marry him. By this time, Robert had gotten his visa extended for six months and he was writing free-lance stories for American newspapers and magazines. I agreed. We had nothing to lose by getting married.

The next morning Robert took his passport and I took mine and we made our way to the marriage office. There were no flowers; there was no wedding dress; there was nothing. The ceremony lasted just ten minutes. We handed to the man conducting the ceremony our passports. He filled in the necessary information, stamped the passports and gave us a certificate of marriage. No witnesses were required. We paid him three rubles and left.

We celebrated our marriage by going to the Café National, the fanciest and most expensive café in Soviet Russia. Thereafter, we went our separate ways; Robert returned to his residence and I returned to mine. It would be another five months before we were able to live as husband and wife and then we lived in a room that Gordon Kashin, an American correspondent, let us use in his three-room apartment.

When the day arrived to meet with the militia who had summoned me, Robert walked with me to the headquarters of the militia. He wanted to go with me inside the building but I told him not to. I feared that he too might be arrested. I left him standing outside. He had turned pale, gray pale. Even his lips were pale. I don't know how I looked but I was certain that I would never see Robert again. Only God knows how horrible I felt.

Inside the building, I walked into a foul-smelling office and showed my summons to a man sitting there. He told me to sit down and wait to be called. I saw four other women sitting there and by the expressions on their faces I could tell that they were experiencing the same nightmare. The four women were called before me and each disappeared into the next office, never to come back.

Finally, the man called out my name, "Nila Ivanovna Shevko." In the next office, I was given a long questionnaire. It asked for my last name, my Christian name, my date of birth, my birthplace, my husband's name and his occupation and so on and so on.

When I filled in my husband's name and occupation, I wrote "Robert Magidoff, American correspondent."

When the man saw my husband's name on the questionnaire, he disappeared into the chief's office. He returned three minutes later and asked me politely to come back in a week and not to leave Moscow before the second interview.

The passing of the week seemed to take forever but when I returned, I was received immediately by the chief officer. "The most horrible thing has happened," he said. "It's all a terrible, terrible mistake you being asked to come here." He then took the summons with my name written on it and tore it into little pieces. "I most humbly apologize for such a stupid blunder."

"You mean I'm free?" I asked, scarcely able to believe my ears.

"Of course. Of course. You may travel where you wish, that is inside the Soviet Union. And I do hope you will try to explain to your husband, it was all a mistake."

I rejoined Robert who was waiting for me outside on the street. I ran to him, put my arms around him and cried, "I'm free! I'm free! I can go anyplace!"

The following paragraphs are the authors' comments:

After Germany invaded the Soviet Union on June 22, 1941, Robert wanted to send Nila to the United States and out of harm's way. With that in mind,

Robert contacted the American ambassador to the Soviet Union, Lawrence Steinhardt. Days later, Steinhardt called Robert with some good news. "I think we have succeeded in getting permission for Nila to go to the United States. We have arranged with the Russians to exchange her [Nila] and Pauline Habicht for two loads of high-octane gas." Pauline was the wife of Herman Habicht, the assistant chief of the United Press Bureau. Thirteen years later, Robert learned that Nila and Pauline and several other people were exchanged not for high-octane gas but for a prominent Russian who was being detained in the United States.

Robert remained in Moscow working as an American correspondent, initially for the Associated Press and then as chief of the NBC (National Broadcasting Corporation) bureau.

After World War II, Nila returned to Moscow and to her husband. However, she and Robert left the Soviet Union after Robert was accused by the Soviet government of being an American spy. They both returned to the United States and freedom.

## NOTE

1. Willie Snow Ethridge. *Nila: Her Story As Told to Willie Snow Ethridge* (New York: Keedick Press, 1956), 1–241.

# Bibliography

Гильди Л.А. Расстрелы, ссылки, мученья. Санкт-Петербург, 1996. 312 стр.

Adamovich, Ales, and Daniil Granin. *A Book of the Blockade.* Translated by Hilda Perham. Moscow: Raduga Publishers, 1983.

Andreyev, Catherine. *Vlasov and the Russian Liberation Movement: Soviet Reality and émigré theories.* Cambridge: Cambrige University Press, 1987.

Brown, Edward J. *Russian Literature since the Revolution.* Cambridge, Massachusetts: Harvard Press, 1982.

Carell, Paul. *Sorched Earth: The Russian—German War, 1943–1944.* Translated by Eewald Osers. Boston: Little, Brown and Company, 1970.

Carleton, Gregory. *The Politics of Reception: Critical Constructions of Mikhail Zoshchenko.* Evanston, Illinois: Northwestern University Press, 1998.

Chew, Allen F. *An Atlas of Russian History: Eleven Centuries of Changing Borders.* New Haven: Yale University Press, 1976.

Clarkson, Jesse D. *A History of Russia.* New York: Random House, Inc., 1961.

Deutscher, I. *Stalin: A Political Biography.* Oxford, England: Oxford University Press, 1949.

Fedeyev, Alexander. *Leningrad in the Days of the Blockade.* Translated by R.D. Charques. Wesport, Connecticut: Greenwood Press, Publishers, 1971.

Fisher, Klaus P. *Nazi Germany, A New History.* New York: The Continuum Publishing Company, 1995.

Fischer, Louis, ed. *Thirteen Who Fled.* New York: Harper and Brothers, 1949.

Goure, Leon. *The Siege of Leningrad.* Stanford, California: Standford University Press, 1962.

Karasev, A.V. *Leningradtsy v gody blokady.* Moscow: Izdatelstvo Adademii Nauk USSR, 1959.

Kislitsyn, Nikolai, and Vassily Zubakov. *Leningrad Does Not Surrender.* Translated by Barry Jones. Moscow: Progress Publishers, 1989.

Kitchen, Martin. *A World in Flames.* New York: Longman Inc., 1990.

Lomagin, Nikita. *The Unknown Blockade.* Moscow: Hower Institution on War, Revolution and Peace, 2002. (In Russian).

Losev, A. *On the Firing Line.* Luga: Luga Publication, 2005. (In Russian).

Magayev, Svetlana, and Albert Pleysier. *Surviving the Blockade of Leningrad.* Translated and edited by Alexey Vinogradov. Lanham, Maryland: University Press of America, Inc., 2006.

Magidoff, Nila, and Willie Snow Ethridge. *Nila: Her Story as Told to Willie Snow Ethridge.* New York: Keedick Press, 1956.

Moss, Walter G. *A History of Russia.* New York: The McGraw-Hill Companies, Inc., 1997.

Newton, Steven H. *Retreat from Leningrad: Army Group North 1944/1945.* Atglen, Pennsylvania: Schiffer Publishing Ltd., 1995.

Pavlov, Dmitri V. *Leningrad 1941: The Blockade.* Translated by John Clinton Adams. Chicago: The University of Chicago Press, 1965.

Payne, Robert. *The Life and Death of Lenin.* New York: Simon and Schuster, Inc., 1964.

Pohl, J. Otto. *Ethnic Cleansing in the USSR, 1937–1949.* Westport, Connecticut: Greenwood Press, 1999.

Riasanovsky, Nicholas V. *A History of Russia.* London: Oxford University Press, 1969.

Seaton, Albert. *The Russo—German War 1941–45.* New York: Praeger Publishers, Inc., 1970.

Serge, victor, and Natalia Sedova Trotsky. *The Life and Death of Leon Trotsky.* Translated by Arnold J. Pomerans. Chicago, Illinois: Haymarket Books, 2015.

Skomorovsky, Boris, and E.G., Morris. *The Sierge of Leningrad.* New York: E.P. Dutton and Company, Inc., 1944.

Skrjabina, Elena. *Siege and Survival.* Translated by Norman Luxenburg. New York: Pinnacle Books, Inc., 1973.

Stalin, Joseph. *Leninism. Vol. II.* New York: International Publishers, 1933.

Tikhonov, Nikolai. *The Defense of Leningrad.* London: Hutchinson and Co., Ltd., no date.

Trotsky, Leon. *My Life: An Attempt at an Autobiography.* New York: Pathfinder Press, Inc., 1970.

Vinogradov, A.V., and A. Pleysier. *Bitva za Leningrad v sud' bakh zhitelel goroda I oblasti: vospominahiiy a zashchitnikov I zhitelei blokadnogo goroda I okkupirovannykh territorii.* Saint Petersburg, Russia: Saint Petersburg State University Press, 2005.

Werth, Alexander. *Leningrad.* London: Hamish Hamilton, 1944.

_____. *Russia at War 1941–1945.* New York: E.P. Dutton and Co., Inc., 1964.

# Documents

## DOCUMENT 1: ARTICLE 58 OF THE
## RUSSIAN SOVIET FEDERATIVE SOCIALIST
## REPUBLIC (RSFSR) PENAL CODE (1934)

Article 58 of the Russian SFSR Penal Code was put in force on February 25, 1927, to arrest those suspected of counterrevolutionary activities. It was revised several times. In particular, its Article 58-1 was updated by the listed sub-articles and put in force on June 8, 1934.

The article identified formally the enemies of the workers (enemies of the people). These enemies were subject to articles 58–2 — 58–13. Those who were subject to 58–1 were traitors guilty of "treason" and those who were subject to 58–14 were saboteurs guilty of "sabotage."

Penal codes of other republics of the Soviet Union also had articles of similar nature.

The following translation was done by Hugo S. Cunningham and copyrighted in 1999:

58-1. "Counterrevolutionary" is understood as any action directed toward the overthrow, subversion, or weakening of the power of worker-peasant councils or of their chosen (according to the Constitution of the USSR and constitutions of union republics) worker-peasant government of the USSR, union and autonomous republics, or toward the subversion or weakening of the external security of the USSR and the fundamental economic, political, and national gains of the proletarian revolution.

58-1a. Treason to the motherland, ie. Acts done by citizens of the USSR in damage to the military power of the USSR, its national sovereignty, or the inviolability of its territory, such as: espionage, betrayal of military or state secrets, crossing to the side of the enemy, flight (by surface or air) abroad, shall be punishable by—the supreme measure of criminal punishment—shooting with confiscation of all property, or with mitigating circumstances—deprivation of liberty for a term of 10 years with confiscation of all property [20 July 1934 (SU No 30, Art. 173)]

> ///Translator's note—The Russian letters "SU" in the previous line do n.o.t. stand for "Soviet Union," which would be "SS" ("Sovetsky Soyuz") in Russian. They m.i.g.,h.t. stand for "Spetsial'ny Ukaz" ("special decree"), but that is only a guess. –HSC///

58-1b. The same crimes, perpetrated by military personnel, are punishable by the supreme measure of criminal punishment—

shooting with confiscation of all property [20 July 1923 (SU No 30, art. 173)]

58-1v. In case of flight (by surface or air) across the border by a military member, the adult members of his family, if they in any way aided the preparation or carrying-out of treason, or only knew about it and failed to report it to authorities, shall be punishable by—

deprivation of liberty for a term of 5 to 10 years, with confiscation of all property.

Remaining adult members of the family of the traitor, living together with him or as his dependents at the moment of the perpetration of the crime, shall be deprived of voting rights and exiled to remote districts of Siberia for 5 years. [20 July 1934 (SU No 30, art 173)]

58-1. Failure by a military member to denounce preparations or the carrying-out of treason shall be punishable by—

deprivation of liberty for 10 years.

Such failure to denounce by other citizens (not military) shall be punished according to article 58–12. [20 July 1934 (SU No 30, art. 173)]

58-2. Armed uprising or incursion with counterrevolutionary purposes on Soviet territory by armed bands, seizure of power in the center or areas with the same purposes, or, in particular, with the purpose of forcibly severing from the USSR and an individual union republic, any part of its territory, or of breaking agreements between the USSR and foreign states, shall be punishable by—

the supreme measure of social defense—shooting, or proclamation as an enemy of the workers, with confiscation or property and with deprivation of citizenship of the union republic, and likewise of citizenship of the Soviet Union and perpetual expulsion beyond the borders of the USSR, with the allowance under extenuating circumstances of reduction to deprivation of liberty for a term of no less than three years, with confiscation of all or part of one's property [6 June 1927 (SU No 49, art 330)].

58-3. Dealings for counterrevolutionary purposes with a foreign state or its individual representatives, and likewise aiding by whatever means a foreign state, engaged in war with the USSR, or conducting against the USSR a struggle by means of intervention or blockade, shall be punishable by—

measures of social defense, indicated in article 58–2 of this code [6 July 1927 (SU No 49, art 333)].

58-4. The offering of whatever kind of aid to that part of the international bourgeoisie, which, not recognizing the equal rights of a Communist system replacing a Capitalist system, exerts itself for its overthrow, and likewise to public groups and organizations, being under the influence of or directly organized by that bourgeoisie, in the carrying out of hostile activities toward the USSR, shall be punishable by—

deprivation of liberty for a term not less than three years with confiscation of all or part of one's property, with an increase, in especially aggravating circumstances, up to the supreme measure of social defense—shooting or declaration to be an enemy of the workers, with deprivation of citizenship of one's union republic, and, likewise, citizenship of the USSR and expulsion beyond the borders of the USSR forever, with confiscation of property [6 June 1927 (SU No 49, art. 330)].

58-5. adherence to a foreign state or any public groups in it, by means of relations with its representatives, use of false documents or other means, toward a declaration of war, armed intervention in the affairs of the USSR or other unfriendly actions, eg: blockade, seizure of state property of the USSR or of union republics, the breaking of diplomatic relations, the breaking of treaties concluded with the USSR, etc., shall be punishable by—

measures of social defense, indicated in article 58–2 of this code [6 June 1927 (SU No 49, art. 330)].

58-6. Espionage, ie. The transmittal, seizure, or collection, with the purpose of transmittal, of information, being a specially kept state secret due to its content, to foreign governments, counterrevolutionary organizations, and private individuals, shall be punishable by—

deprivation of liberty for a term not less than three years, with confiscation of all or part of one's property, or in those cases where the espionage brought or could bring especially severe consequences for the interests of the USSR—the supreme measure of social defense shooting or proclamation as an enemy of the workers with deprivation of citizenship of one's union republic and, likewise, of citizenship of the USSR and expulsion beyond the borders of the USSR forever with confiscation of property.

Transmittal, seizure, or collection for purpose of transmittal of economic information, not consisting by its content of specially preserved state secrets, but not subject to publication either due to direct legal prohibition, or due to the decision of the management of the department, institution, or enterprise, whether for reward or for free, to organizations and persons listed above, shall be punishable by—

deprivation of liberty for a term up to three years [6 June 1927 (SU No 49, art. 330)].

Footnote 1: That information is considered a specially preserved state secret, which is enumerated in a special list, confirmed by the Council of People's Commissars of the USSR in coordination with the councils of people's commissars for the union republics and published in a general notice [6 June 1927 (SU No 49, art 330)].

Footnote 2: Concerning espionage by persons indicated in art. 193-1 of this code ///military personnel///, art. 193–24 of this code remains in force [9 January 1928 (SU No 12, art. 108)].

58-7. The undermining of state production, transport, trade, monetary relations or the credit system, or likewise cooperation, done with counter-revolutionary purposes, by means of corresponding use of state institutions and enterprises or impeding their normal activity, and likewise use of state institutions and enterprises or impeding their activity, done in the interests of former owners or interested capitalist organizations, shall be punishable by –

measures of social defense, indicated in article 58–2 of this code [6 June 1927 (SU No 49, art. 330)].

58-8. The perpetration of terrorist acts, directed against representatives of Soviet authority or activists of revolutionary workers' and peasants' organizations, and participation in the performance of such acts, even by persons not belonging to a counterrevolutionary organization, shall be punishable by—

measures of social defense, indicated in article 58–2 of this code [6 June 1927 (SU No 49, art. 330)].

58-9. Destruction or damage with a counterrevolutionary purpose by explosion, arson, or other means of railroad or other routes and means of transportation, means of public communication, water conduits, public depots and other structures, or state and community property, shall be punishable by—

measures of social defense, indicated in art. 58–2 of this code [6 June 1927 (SU No 49, art. 330)].

58-10. Propaganda or agitation, containing a call for the overthrow, subversion, or weakening of Soviet authority or for the carrying out of other counterrevolutionary crimes (art. 58–2 to 58–9 of this code), and likewise the distribution or preparation or keeping of literature of this nature shall be punishable by—

deprivation of liberty for a term not less than six months.

The same action during mass disturbances, or with the use of religious or nationalist prejudices of the masses, or in a war situation, or in areas proclaimed to be in a war situation, shall be punishable by—

measure of social defense, indicated in art. 58–2 of this code [6 June 1927 (SU No 49, art. 330)].

58-11. Any type of organizational activity, directed toward the preparation or carrying out of crimes indicated in this chapter, and likewise participation in an organization, formed for the preparation or carrying out of one of the crimes indicated in this chapter, shall be punishable by—

measures of social defense, indicated in the corresponding articles of this code [6 June 1927 (SU No 49, art. 330)].

58-12. Failure to denounce a counterrevolutionary crime, reliably known to be in preparation or carried out, shall be punishable by—

deprivation of liberty for a term not less than six months. [6 June 1927 (SU No 49, art. 330)].

58-13. Active participation or active fighting against the working class and revolutionary movement, manifested in a responsible or secret position in the tsarist regime, or with counterrevolutionary governments in a period of civil war, shall be punishable by—

> measures of social defense, indicated in art. 58–2 of this code [6 June 1927 (SU No 49, art. 330)].

58-14. Counterrevolutionary sabotage, ie. Conscious failure to perform some defined duties or intentionally negligent fulfillment of them, with the special purpose of weakening the authority of the government and functioning of the state apparatus, shall be punishable by—

> deprivation of liberty for a term not less than one year, with confiscation of all or part of one's property, with an increase, in especially aggravating circumstances, to the supreme measure of social defense—shooting with confiscation of property [6 Jun 1927 (SU No 49, art. 330)].

## DOCUMENT 2: THE ORDER OF SUPREME HIGH COMMAND GENERAL HEADQUARTERS FROM THE 16TH OF AUGUST, 1941 #270 "REGARDING THE RESPONSIBILITY OF THE MILITARY POPULATION FOR SURRENDER AND LEAVING WEAPONS TO THE ENEMY."

August 16, 1941

Not only our friends admit but our enemies are forced to admit as well that in our liberation war with German-Fascist invaders, the units of the Red Army, the vast majority of them, the commanders and the commissars, are conducting themselves impeccably, courageously, and at times straight out heroically. Even those units of the army that were accidentally detached from the army and surrounded, maintain the spirit of resilience and courage, do not surrender, attempt to inflict ever more damage upon the enemy, and break out of the encirclement. It is known that certain units of our army, upon having been surrounded by the enemy, use every opportunity to defeat the enemy, and disentangle.

While near the 10th army near Belostok that was surrounded by German-Fascist forces, deputy commander of the Western Front Lieutenant General Boldin organized the Red Army units left behind the enemy's lines into squads that fought behind the enemy lines for 45 days and broke through to the main forces of the Western Front. They destroyed the headquarters of 2 German regiments, 26 tanks, 1,049 passenger, transport, and staff vehicles, 147 motorcycles, 5 batteries, 4 mortars, 15 mounted machine-guns, 8 hand-held machine-guns, 1 airplane at the airfield, and an aerial bomb depot.

Over a thousand German soldiers and officers were killed. On August 11, Lieutenant General Boldin attacked the Germans from behind, broke through the German front and, uniting with our troops, broke out of the encirclement 1,654 armed Red Army soldiers and commanders, 103 of whom were wounded.

Commissar of the 8th mechanized corps, Brigade Commissar Popel and the commander of the 406th infantry regiment Lieutenant Colonel Novikov by assault led 1,778 armed people out of the encirclement. In the hard-fought combat with the Germans, Novikov-Popel's group walked 650 kilometers inflicting great losses behind the enemy's lines.

Commander of the 3rd army Lieutenant General Kuznetsov and a member of the War Council Army Commissar of the 2nd rank Biryukov by assault led 498 armed Red Army soldiers and unit commanders of the 3rd army out of encirclement, and organized the disentanglement of the 108th and the 64th infantry divisions.

All these and other numerous similar acts testify to the persistence of our troops, and the high morale of our soldiers, commanders, and commissars.

But we cannot conceal the fact that recently, there have been several deplorable acts of surrender. Certain generals set a bad example to our troops.

Commander of the 28th army Lieutenant General Kachalov who together with his headquarters troops was encircled, demonstrated cowardice and yielded himself prisoner to the German fascists. However, the headquarters of Kachalov's group fought their way out of the encirclement. Lieutenant General Kachalov chose to surrender, chose to defect to the enemy.

Lieutenant General Ponedelin who commanded the 12th army, when surrounded by the enemy had a good opportunity to break through to our troops the way the overwhelming majority of his army units did. But Podelin did not display the necessary persistence and will to win. He gave in to panic, turned coward, and yielded himself prisoner to the enemy. He defected to the enemy, thus committing a crime before his Motherland as a violator of the military oath.

Commander of the 13th infantry corps Brigadier General Kirillov who was surrounded by the German-fascist troops instead of fulfilling his duty to his Motherland and organizing the units entrusted to him to resiliently hold off the enemy and break out of the encirclement, defected from the army and surrendered himself to the enemy. As a result of that, the units of the 13th infantry corps were defeated and several of them surrendered without any serious resistance.

It is important to point out that in all the aforementioned cases of surrender, the members of Army War Councils, commanders, political workers, counterintelligence agents that were encircled displayed unacceptable confusion, deplorable cowardice, and did not even attempt to prevent the cowardly Kachalovs, Ponedelins, Kirillovs, and others from yielding themselves prisoners to the enemy.

These despicable acts of surrender to our sworn enemy demonstrate that, in the Red Army which is bravely and selflessly protecting its Soviet Motherland from the dishonorable invaders, there exists weak, fainthearted, cowardly elements. And these cowardly elements exist not only among the soldiers, but among the command officers as well. It is known that some commanders and political workers do not only fail to set the example of courage, resilience, and love to the Motherland, but do the exact opposite—hide in the cracks, putter around the executive offices, do not see and do not watch over the battlefield, and at the sign of the first difficulty in battle, they quail before the enemy, tear off the insignia, and defect from the battlefield.

In our Red Army, can we tolerate the cowards that defect to the enemy and yield themselves prisoners or the fainthearted commanders who tear off their insignia and defect behind the enemy's line at the first problem at the front? No, we cannot! If we let these cowards and defectors do what they please, they will enervate our army which will lead to the destruction of our Motherland in no time. Cowards and defectors need to be destroyed.

Can we consider the commanders that hide in the cracks during combat, that do not see the battlefield, that do not watch the battle, yet imagine themselves to be commanders of regiments and battalions to be actual commanders? No, we cannot! These are not regiment and battalion commanders, these are impostors.

If we set these impostors loose, in a very short time, they will turn our army into one big executive office. Such impostors need to be removed from power, demoted, reduced to the ranks, and if necessary shot on the spot, and brave and courageous people among junior commanding officers or soldiers should be promoted to take their place.

I hereby order:

To consider commanders and political workers that tear off their insignia during combat and defect behind the enemy's lines or surrender to the enemy to be malicious defectors, whose families are subjects to arrest as the families of the violators of the military oath and defectors who betrayed their Motherland.

To compel all the senior commanders and commissars to shoot such defecting commanding officers on the spot.

To compel units and detachments that are surrounded by the enemy to selflessly fight as long as possible, to protect the material equipment like the apple of one's eye, to break through to our army behind the enemy's lines, defeating the fascist dogs.

To compel all military personnel regardless of one's rank to demand that the senior officer, if in encirclement, fight as long as possible to break through to our troops, and if such officer or a group of soldiers would choose to surrender rather than holding off the enemy, to destroy them by all possible means, ground or air; and that the families of the surrendered soldiers to be deprived of the government stipend and aid.

To compel division commanders and commissars to immediately remove from power the battalion and regiment commanders that hide in the cracks during combat and are afraid of controlling the action on the battlefield, to demote them, to reduce them to the ranks and, if necessary, to shoot them on the spot, and to promote brave and courageous people among junior commanding officers or soldiers who have distinguished themselves to take their place.

To read this order in all companies, squadrons, batteries, air squadrons, brigades and headquarters.

Supreme High Command of the Red Army General Headquarters
Chairman of the State Committee of Defense
J. Stalin
Vice-Chairman of the State Committee of Defense V. Molotov
Marshal of the Soviet Union S. Budenniy
Marshal of the Soviet Union K. Voroshilov
Marshal of the Soviet Union S. Timoshenko
Marshal of the Soviet Union B. Shaposhnikov
Army General G. Zhukov

# Glossary

## ABORTION

On May 26, 1936, the draft of a law "On the Protection of Motherhood and Childhood" was published in Soviet newspapers with an appeal for public discussion of its contents. The draft included measures that were aimed at "combating light-minded attitudes towards the family and family obligations," tightening restrictions on divorce and increasing the prestige of mothers of many children. The new official attitudes towards the above issues reflected a major shift from the more liberal marriage law of 1926 which had replaced the even more radical legislation dating back to the early 1920s.

By the mid-1930s the declining birth in the Soviet Union became a major concern for the leadership in the Russian Communist Party. The concern doomed the old abortion law. For Stalin, giving birth was "a great and honorable duty" which was "not a private affair but one of great social importance." Henceforth, Soviet women would have to carry out the double burden of holding a job outside the home and working in the home raising children. The draft proclaimed that "only under conditions of socialism, where . . . [a] woman is an equal member of society . . . is it possible seriously to organize the struggle against abortions by prohibitive laws as well as by other means." The draft permitted abortions only in cases when the continuation of pregnancy threatened the life of the pregnant mother.

Opposition to the proposed legislation came from many quarters but was particularly prominent among young urban women. Their objections to the draft typically were not based on a woman's right to control her body but rather on the difficulties that bearing and raising children would impose on their pursuit of a career and on available living space. There were other concerns as well. Except for minor changes, the draft was approved by the Central Executive Committee and the Council of People's Commissars. It went into effect as legislation on June 27, 1936. The number of officially recorded abortions dropped from 1.9 million in 1935 to 570,000 in 1937.

But in time the number of abortions began to climb and officially it reached 755,000 in 1939.


## ANDREY VLASOV

Andrey Vlasov was a Red Army general. He was captured by the enemy trying to lift the siege of Leningrad. As a prisoner of war, he defected to Hitler's Germany and formed and headed the Russian Liberation Army.


## BLACK RAVEN

The Black Raven was a black vehicle consisting of two compartments, the driver's cab at the front and a large van at the rear. The only window to the van was near the top of the rear door. In front of the window there were steel bars. Inside the van, there were two long benches, one along each side of the van. The NKVD agents who conducted arrests would transport the victims in Black Ravens.


## COMMISSAR

A commissar was a Russian Communist Party official assigned to a military unit to teach Party principles and policies and to ensure Party loyalty.

Commissars were introduced into the Red Army shortly after it was formed in 1918. They represented the Communist Party. Their primary function was to supervise the former Czarist military officers who were employed by Vladimir Lenin's regime. In addition, they were used by Lenin's regime to spread its principles and philosophy.

During World War Two commissars were assigned to military officers in the Red Army and to guerrilla commanders. They were the eyes and ears of officers. They had the authority to decorate or rescind decoration. They had the power to judge individuals and discharge them from the military or to pardon them. Commissars that were assigned to guerrilla commanders were not given such authority or power.


## ICON

An icon in the Russian Orthodox Church is generally an image of Jesus the son of God or the Virgin Mary or some other saint that has been painted on a small or large smoothed wooden panel. The Church teaches that a saint in Heaven will hear the requests that are expressed in prayers by a worshiper, and the requests are then brought by the saint to Jesus or God. An icon bearing the image of a saint is designed to assist the worshipper by helping her or him visualize the saint.

## KOMSOMOL

Membership in the Komsomol (The Young Communist League) was made up of young people between the ages of fifteen and twenty-eight. Komsomol membership among students in institutions of higher learning was usually high because membership would help a person gain admission into these institutions. Although the age limit for membership was twenty-eight, provision was made in the Komsomol statutes for officers to remain in the organization beyond that age.

Komsomol members were exposed to intense ideological indoctrination and were expected to participate in all aspects of Soviet society. Members would offer their services to the armed forces if the State called for recruits in an emergency situation. They were also expected to work in a factory or on a collective farm whenever there was a shortage of labor.

Members who entered the military or who joined an industrial or an agricultural force were responsible for the political education of their co-workers who were of the same age group. Komsomol members had been trained for this responsibility during Komsomol meetings which were mainly discussions and lectures on Marxist-Leninist ideology.

Komsomol members performed an important surveillance function in society. They frequently inspected enterprises and did this usually without prior warning. They sought to expose corruption, waste and inefficiency in management and laziness and tardiness among workers. The surveillance function of the Komsomol was even more extensive in institutions of higher learning. The activities of students who were members were carefully observed. Failure to meet the Komsomol standards of behavior could result in expulsion from the organization. Komsomol members with a university education were an important source for recruitment for the Russian Communist Party.

# NIKITA KHRUSHCHEV'S SPEECH
# TO THE TWENTIETH CONGRESS OF THE
# COMMUNIST PARTY OF THE SOVIET UNION

At the Twentieth Congress of the Communist Party held in February 1956, Nikita Khrushchev gave a long speech in which he denounced Joseph Stalin. He described, in detail, to startled Communist delegates the horrible acts of cruelty that were committed at the orders of Stalin during the purges of the 1930s. Thousands of devoted Communists had been liquidated and many top military leaders had been executed, which weakened gravely the Red Army. He accused Stalin of trusting Hitler and jeopardizing the country's defense. He claimed that Stalin's wartime failings caused the deaths of countless Soviet troops. Further, Khrushchev explained how Stalin had "supported the glorification of his own person with all conceivable methods." The speech left many delegates in a state of shock and as details of the speech became known to the Soviet public, there were other responses. Many people were distressed at the attack on the man they had worshipped so long. There were also many who were not surprised; they had suspected that Stalin was something less than godlike.

# NKVD

The Narodnyy Konissariat Vnutrennikh Del (People's Commissariat for Internal Affairs) was better known as the NKVD. Its origin was in Cheka (Extraordinary Commission) established in December 1917 as a temporary police force empowered to investigate counterrevolutionary activities. Cheka conducted a campaign of terror against the propertied classes and enemies of Bolshevism. Cheka's functions were transferred, in 1922, to the State Political Administration, or GPU, which was less powerful than its predecessor. In 1923, the United Political Administration, or OGPU, was created, and during its tenure, which ended in 1934, repression against the people lessened. The secret police again acquired vast punitive powers when they became, in 1934, the People's Commissariat for Internal Affairs, or NKVD. The NKVD was not subject to the control of the Russian Communist Party nor was it restricted by law. It was the instrument that Joseph Stalin used in the 1930s against the people he wanted removed from the Party and arrested in the country. The NKVD remained one of the most powerful and feared Soviet institutions throughout the Stalinist period.

# OCTOBER REVOLUTION

Vladimir Lenin and his Bolsheviks removed from power the Provisional Government in Russia on November 7, 1917, according to the Gregorian calendar. The removal was called the October Socialist Revolution. In Russia the Gregorian calendar was adopted after the October Socialist Revolution (so named because it took place in October 1917 in the Julian calendar). On January 24, 1918, the Council of People's Commissars decreed that January 31,1918 (Julian calendar) was to be followed by February 14, 1918 (Gregorian calendar). Thereafter the Russians used the Gregorian calendar.

# ORDER NO. 227

During the first months of the Great Patriotic War the Red Army of the Soviet Union suffered heavy losses along with mass retreats and desertions. In response Joseph Stalin acting as the People's Commissar of Defense issued Order No. 227 on July 28, 1942. It was intended to re-establish discipline in the Red Army in the battle against the invading armies of Adolf Hitler's Germany. The order led to the formation of penal military battalions composed of sentenced soldiers, political prisoners and others that the State considered expendable. A large number of Red Army soldiers who retreated without orders were reorganized into penal battalions. The order became known for its line "Not one step back!"

The order established that each Soviet military front must create one to three penal battalions. They were to be sent to the most dangerous sections of the front lines. By the end of 1942 there were 24,993 troops serving in penal battalions and that number increased to 177,694 in 1943. The number decreased over the next two years to 143,457 and 81,766 soldiers in 1944 and 1945, respectively.

Order No. 227 also directed that each army create "blocking detachments" at the rear. They were to shoot "panic-mongers and cowards," soldiers who retreated without orders to retreat. In the first three months after their creation, the "blocking detachments" shot 1,000 troops and sent 24,000 soldiers to penal battalions. The "blocking detachments" were intended to galvanize the morale of the Red Army and emphasize patriotism. They had a generally detrimental effect and were not consistently implemented by military commanders who viewed diverting troops to create "blocking detachments" as a waste of manpower. On October 29, 1944, the "blocking detachments" were disbanded by Order No. 349 of the People's Commissar of Defense (Joseph Stalin) citing, as justification, the changed situation at the military fronts.

# RED ARMY

The October Socialist Revolution in 1917 brought Vladimir Lenin and his followers to power in Russia. Following the revolution, Lenin disbanded the Czarist Russian Army and in January 1918 the newly created Soviet government ordered the formation of the Red Army of Workers and Peasants. Leon Trotsky, the People's Commissar for War, was assigned in March 1918 to create and be the head of the Red Army. The army had to be organized quickly as it was needed to fight the White Army that had been formed within Russia to remove Lenin and his Communists from power. Trotsky recruited a large number of officers from the Czarist Russian Army. When he was criticized for this, he argued that it would be impossible to win the Russian Civil War without the employment of experienced army officers. At the beginning of its existence, the Red Army was a volunteer army, but losses during the civil war forced the Soviet government, in May 1918, to introduce conscription. At the end of the Russian Civil War, in 1921, there were over five million men in the Red Army. The majority of the soldiers were released from military service after the civil war; some 600,000 men were retained to form a regular army.

When Adolf Hitler came to power in Germany in 1933 the Soviet government led by Joseph Stalin decided to increase the size of the Red Army. By 1935 the army had grown to 1,300,000 men. To every unit of the army was assigned a political commissar who was given the authority to override the decisions made by unit commanders if the decisions were in opposition to the principles of the Russian Communist Party. The army also included members of the NKVD whose role it was to ensure that the army remained loyal to Stalin and his administration. By 1941 the Red Army had grown to three million men (three hundred divisions). Most of the men served in un-mechanized rifle divisions. The infantry was supported by horse-drawn artillery and a cavalry. The army also had two tank corps. It was the Red Army that would combat the Germans and the Finns as they invaded Soviet Russia in June 1941.

# SMERSH

SMERSH was an acronym for Smert Shpionam which is translated Death to Spies. It was founded on April 14, 1943, and was given the name SMERSH by Joseph Stalin who rejected the originally proposed title, Death to German Spies. Stalin believed that the new intelligence service should concern itself with all spies.

The duties of SMERSH were extensive. Its agents were responsible for uncovering spies, saboteurs and subversives in the Red Army. They were charged with ensuring the protection of military factories, military goods and military shipments. They were given the task of screening all liberated Soviet prisoners-of-war and all Soviet citizens who were liberated by the Red Army. SMERSH agents were ordered to identify German spies and collaborators in areas that had been liberated or were occupied by the Red Army. The agents of SMERSH and the NKVD often worked together during the Great Patriotic War. In May 1946, SMERSH was disbanded and its duties were transferred to the Ministry of State Security.

## SOVIET REHABILITATION

The term "rehabilitation" in the Soviet Union referred to the political and social restoration of a person who had been repressed or criminally prosecuted without due basis. "Rehabilitation" restored the person to the state of acquittal. In many cases, "rehabilitation" was posthumous, as thousands of victims had been executed or had died in prison labor camps.

## THE MARSEILLE

"La Marseillaise" is the national anthem of France. The song was written in 1792 by Claude Joseph Rouget de Lisle. The French National Convention adopted it as the republic's anthem in 1795. The anthem's evocative melody and lyrics have led to its widespread use as a song of revolution.

## UNION OF SOVIET WRITERS

The Union of Soviet Writers was formed by the Central Committee of the Russian Communist Party on April 23, 1932. All other literary organizations were dissolved. Writers who did not belong to the official union, found it almost impossible to get their work published.

# Appendix

## *Maps and Photograph*

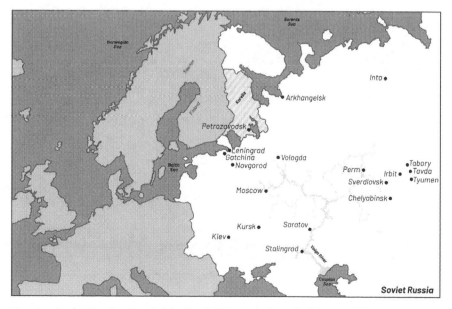

Map 1.  Soviet Russia. Created by Sarah Bittner and used with permission.

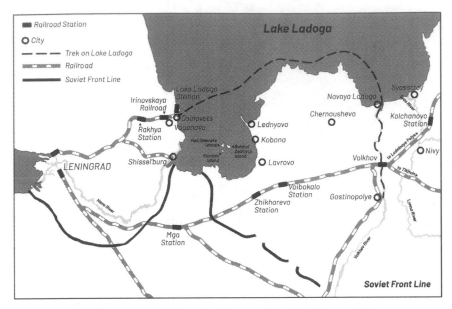

Map 2. Lake Ladoga. Created by Sarah Bittner and used with permission.

Olga Minkevich in her apartment in St. Petersburg. Photograph taken by Alexey Vinogradov.

# Index

# About the Authors

**Alexey Vinogradov** earned his Ph.D. in archaeology at Leningrad State University. He has been the acting chairman of the Research Center for Archaeology, Historical Sociology, and Cultural Heritage of the St. Petersburg State University in St. Petersburg, Russia.

**Albert Pleysier** was born in Utrecht, the Netherlands. He earned his Ph.D. in European history from West Virginia University and is currently a professor of history at Piedmont University in Demorest, Georgia.

## BOOKS BY THE AUTHORS

*Bitva za Leningrad v sud' bakh zhitelel goroda I oblasti: vospominahiiy a zashchitnikov I zhitelei blokadnogo goroda I okkupirovan-nykh territorii (The Battle of Leningrad: Memories of its Citizens and People in the Occupied Surrounding Areas)*, Saint Petersburg State University Press, 2005

*Surviving the Blockade of Leningrad*, University Press of America, 2006

*The Women of Ismaelovka: A Soviet Union Collective Farm in Siberia*, University Press of America, 2007

*Frozen Tears: The Blockade and Battle of Leningrad*, University Press of America, 2008

*Unlocked Memories: Young Russians under German Rule*, University Press of America, 2011

*Henry VIII and the Anabaptists*, University Press of America, 2014

*Exiled to Stalin's Prisons*, Hamilton Books, 2019